# A Guide for
# New Public Speaking Teachers
## Building Toward Success

**Calvin L. Troup**
*Duquesne University*

Allyn and Bacon
Boston  London  Toronto  Sydney  Tokyo  Singapore

Copyright © 1999 by Allyn & Bacon
A Pearson Education Company
160 Gould Street
Needham Heights, Massachusetts 02494

Internet: www.abacon.com

ISBN 0-205-29306-9

Printed in the United States of America

10 9 8 7 6 5 4 3 2 1   03 02 01 00 99

# A Guide for New Public Speaking Teachers: Building Toward Success

## Contents

# Chapter Three: Putting the Plan into Action     47

# Chapter Four:  Dealing With Challenges   82

# Chapter Five: Resource Matrix   93

# Introduction

Teaching public speaking is not rocket science. Rocket science is simpler. It relies on fixed formulas and predictable physical laws and conditions. By contrast, as a public speaking instructor you will deal with human beings learning an ancient art form through which the course of history has been fashioned and refashioned. People have been teaching others to speak publicly for 5,000 years or more. Therefore, as you prepare to teach, you join an ancient tradition in the academy. You may find yourself teaching public speaking with or without broad speaking experience yourself, with or without teaching experience in a college classroom, and with or without a deep theoretical foundation in the field of communication. You may teach the course in any of a number of various instructional circumstances. But whatever the teaching circumstance, your approach to the classroom, your understanding of the special challenges presented by public speaking, and your knowledge of available support will be crucial to your effectiveness.

As you begin, remember that students are resilient. Speakers, even inexperienced ones, are inclined to find their own voice if given the opportunity, including a favorable learning environment, good reasons and good reasoning to accompany their practice of the art, and high expectations from their instructor. Also remember that you must find your own voice as the instructor in your classroom, just as your students must find their voices as speakers. Finally, never forget that you are preparing to teach a **basic public speaking** course. I was privileged to hear Carroll Arnold, a distinguished communication scholar and major contributor to the development of the discipline, share his wisdom with new public speaking instructors in the twilight of his life. His most memorable remarks called for simplicity. He explained that each semester he spent teaching the course, he aimed at only three learning objectives for students: (1) to organize their messages; (2) to adapt their messages to the audience; (3) to speak extemporaneously. Your objectives may vary, but basics, not details, will lead to effectiveness. Students can make significant progress in their public speaking knowledge and ability when you stick to the basics.

## Approach to the Classroom: A Teacher/Scholar Model

You have choices about your orientation toward the classroom. On one hand, you may regard teaching undergraduates as an evil necessary to achieving your scholarly goals. On the other hand, you may regard yourself as an educator who works in different modes but always with the same basic calling, whether in the classroom, library, or study. Practically speaking, communication scholars rarely pursue their research to the exclusion of teaching. Some professors consider teaching introductory courses a waste of time and an unwelcome diversion from their scholarship. However, the best seek out connections between their scholarship and how they teach every course, including the basic public speaking course. Whether you choose to see teaching and scholarship as mutually exclusive activities or as connected and integrated modes of the same vocation, your choice will be reflected in your attitude and performance as a public speaking teacher. The remainder of this teaching manual assumes the second view--a teacher/scholar model—and expects you to be constantly exploring relevant connections between your research and the courses you teach. Make the classroom a site where you can incorporate what you are learning, explore and test emerging thought, and generate new questions through the readings, activities, and assignments you select for the course. As you begin to accomplish the integration of your teaching and scholarship, the quality of each should improve, as should the learning experience of your students.

# The Special Challenges of the Public Speaking Course

Reflect on the basic public speaking class as it was taught at the college or university where you did your bachelor's degree; think over the variety of challenges presented by the course. As an instructor, you will need to take stock of these challenges and prepare yourself to address them. First of all, on many campuses public speaking is a requirement. Therefore, so many people take the course that their **expectations,** informed by the student culture, may rival the expectations set by the department and instructor. Most commonly, students expect to get a good grade in public speaking with a minimal amount of effort. First of all, they know they are taking an introduction to public speaking, an introductory course not ordinarily used to screen out all but the best and the brightest students. Second, many students in the course are not communication majors. They may have a mistaken tendency to view communication as a less serious field of study than their own. Finally, since so many people are required to take public speaking—on some campuses public speaking is a graduation requirement for all students—the difficulty of the course and how to get a good grade in it are part of the campus lore. Not every student will know these factors on the first day of class, but many will find out from talking to friends and acquaintances what to expect from public speaking.

Regardless of expectations, most students come to the course seriously under-prepared, especially compared to their preparation for other introductory courses. From kindergarten on, formal education is primarily an exercise in literacy training: learning to read, write, and figure. Less than half of your students are likely to have had a high school course in public speaking. Many will have performed token oral assignments in English class or some other subject, but without much in the way of systematic training. Some will have public speaking experience. But take a moment to compare how long they have been writing and reading sentences, paragraphs, essays, and books with the corresponding time devoted to critical listening and skill development in presentations of spoken language. Education has made them well acquainted with the written word, but the same education has neglected the spoken word. You will have few exceptions to this rule, which means that you will be teaching college-level literate minds who have a lot of catching up to do in their oral skill development.

You will introduce students to **oral patterns of thought and language**, arts quite foreign to many literate people, at least in an educational context. Their initial inclination will be to write out a speech as if it were an essay, and then read it to the class or memorize it for delivery. When you ask students to speak extemporaneously, you are asking them to awaken latent cognitive skills and develop patterns of thought that they may admire in other speakers but believe to be personally unattainable. Literacy skills may assist in learning about public speaking and in researching speeches. But the design and performance of their presentations must be grounded in remembering and producing the spoken word without memorization, and in understanding how listeners receive the spoken word versus the written word.

As a result, instructors may be tempted to offer a simplistic course oriented toward practice alone, devoting most class sessions to speeches and speaking exercises. Even with minimal instruction, many people will improve their speaking skills dramatically by being forced to speak for a grade a number of times in succession. But when the primary objective becomes making inexperienced speakers feel more comfortable in front of groups, we rob students of the knowledge they need to integrate performance and theory, the why behind the how. The aim of any public speaking course should be to equip students with integrated knowledge and skill in the art, so that they can continue to advance as speakers long after completing the course.

Even when we strike a good balance between instruction and student speaking assignments, speeches must be given in class, which puts instructional time at a premium. In other courses, we routinely assign major course projects to be completed outside of class. However, a well-balanced public speaking course still requires one third to one half of the class sessions for student speeches. Therefore, teachers must maximize the use of class sessions dedicated to instruction and utilize the inherent instructional opportunities in every speaking round.

Finally, in public speaking the instructor not only teaches content, but also models speaking performance. You bear a broader instructional burden in public speaking than in most courses, simply because students should scrutinize how you present yourself and the course material. Thankfully, you will not be expected to perform perfectly, but no public speaking instructor escapes the conscious realization that while we teach public speaking we employ the same skills in the process. If you lack speaking experience, concentrate on practicing what you are preaching. If you possess confidence as a public speaker, draw attention to transferable skills and strategies as you use them, and work to expand your proficiency every time you enter the public speaking classroom.

## The Textbook and Supporting Materials for the Basic Course

Become intimately familiar with your textbook. A textbook is only as good as your ability to recognize and communicate its value to your students. Obviously, in a college classroom your task is to teach public speaking, not merely to review a textbook. But instructors who use a textbook wisely may better help their students overcome the lack of preparation, need for theoretical knowledge, and limited in-class instruction time mentioned previously.  A good textbook serves as a touchstone for students throughout their public speaking experience.

In public speaking, you can weave the textbook into your course to cultivate student learning, without ever giving a "read your book!" speech in class.   The role of the text in your class and how to use it most effectively will be discussed in detail in Chapter Three.  For now, recognize that a good public speaking text can save you substantial amounts of preparation time and enhance the learning process for students inside and outside of class.  Quality publishers like Allyn & Bacon provide extensive support to help you get the most out of the text in your course. This training manual, along with supplements for students that may be required or offered as optional materials,  is only one example of the broad spectrum of resources available to assist your in-class instruction.

If you are using one of the following public speaking texts, Allyn & Bacon places a full range of materials at your disposal to enhance learning for students in your course:

*Public Speaking: An Audience-Centered Approach*, by Steven A. Beebe & Susan J. Beebe.

*Public Speaking in the Age of Diversity*, by Teri Kwal Gamble & Michael W. Gamble.

*Mastering Public Speaking*, by George L. Grice & John F. Skinner.

*Public Speaking: Strategies for Success*, by David Zarefsky.

Each of these texts has been used successfully nationwide.  All four effectively cover the basic principles of public speaking, but do so with distinctive emphases and unique features.  Chapter Five of this manual provides a grid of corresponding activities and exercises you can use to teach basic concepts and principles from each of the textbooks.  Refer to the grid to find additional ideas or specific emphases available in Allyn & Bacon textbooks other than the one adopted for your course.  The grid also identifies supplemental Allyn & Bacon resources like videos of student speeches, videos of famous speakers from the past and the present, and software designed to help students support and organize their speeches.

## The Plan of . . . *Building toward Success*

The basics of public speaking have not changed dramatically over the centuries. However, as the emphases of textbooks reflect, approaches to the course vary widely. Each college or university generates a different cultural setting for the course and serves a different community. Chapter One leads you through an assessment of the **context** for your particular course and choices you must make concerning how to frame your course at this particular moment in the life of your department, institution, and the field of communication. You complete **pre-term preparations** in Chapter Two, which leads you from considering your multiple roles as an instructor, through how a textbook and other resources can support the course, to the structure and final syllabus to be distributed to students. Chapter Three provides a brief introduction to **teaching methods** and **standard instructional components** from which to build an effective class session. The special issues related to the first day of class are considered as are options and strategies for conducting speaking rounds, evaluating speeches, and testing in public speaking courses.

In Chapter Four, you will consider some **routine problems** new instructors face and common questions most of us have asked as we teach public speaking the first time, questions such as: "How do I balance my other responsibilities with my teaching?" "I don't have a bachelor's degree in communication: how can I best handle this assignment?" "How can I maintain a free speech environment regarding religious and ideological positions when I suspect that speakers will seriously offend other class members?" The grid or matrix of **Allyn & Bacon resources** appears in Chapter Five, after a list of the resources referenced on the grid and followed by a series of **sample lesson plans** for core topics taught in most public speaking courses.  The book concludes with a provocative essay by Professor Roderick Hart, reprinted with permission from *Communication Education*, as a catalyst for your consideration and discussion among colleagues.

# Chapter One:
# Framing the Public Speaking Course

Whether you like it or not, teaching involves you in the life of an institution and perhaps several institutions. The public speaking course you teach is located in time and space. Whole histories, traditions, communities, disciplines, and varieties of culture have contributed to the moment you and your students will move through as a class. You will do well to familiarize yourself with the particular constraints and opportunities of the moment in which you will serve as an instructor. You and your students will contribute in some way to the tradition of the public speaking course at your institution. To contribute well demands that you develop a sense for your historical moment. That will mean assessing the current mission of the course in the life of your university, department, and discipline; setting definite objectives for your particular section(s); and grasping the rationale behind conventions incorporated in most public speaking courses today.

## The Course in Your Community

Much of the record we have of public speaking in the ancient world—ordinarily called rhetoric—comes from master scholars of antiquity who earned their living by teaching people to advocate and defend their ideas and selves in their own communities. Of course they argued about methods, ethics, effects, and social implications, which constitutes most of what we have in addition to surviving manuals and lecture notes. Most of them taught and wrote on a great deal more than public speaking as well. The point is, instruction in public speaking seems to predate written history in at least some human civilizations. Early historical records appear with public speaking teachers already on the scene and more-or-less gainfully employed—teaching concepts, methods, and skills inseparable from the local, temporal context.

At various times public speaking instruction has taken the form of training in rhetoric, oratory, or elocution. Sometimes it has been referred to as declamation. In certain times and places in the Western world, courses in public speaking all but evaporated. Rhetorical ideas and skills initially associated with oratory shifted almost entirely to the written word. More recently, the advent of quantitative and qualitative social scientific approaches to communication has further expanded our ideas about public speaking. Although common ideas are woven through the historical tapestry that constitutes the background to your public speaking class, the teaching has truly varied from moment to moment and place to place; people were not all teaching the same thing and merely applying different labels. Public speaking courses reflect and shape the particular needs of the communities in which they emerge as an essential component of liberal higher education. When taught well, public speaking courses can become indispensable to the life of such communities. You must seek to understand the particular community in which your course is offered and frame it clearly for students in terms of the college or university, department, and discipline.

## Institution:  Mission, History, and Student Culture

At one public university, a story is told about how the public speaking course became a graduation requirement for all bachelors' degree candidates. A certain engineering professor was working with an unsurpassed doctoral student. At the end of his work at the university, the new Ph.D. was interviewed for a top industry position in the field. Part of the interview required a presentation of his research, which flopped. He did not get the position. Some time later, when the professor became president of the university, one of his first official acts was to make the basic public speaking course an undergraduate requirement for every student.

What is the mission of the college or university in which you will teach public speaking? How is the mission connected to the history and tradition of the school? The educational missions and histories of institutions vary widely, even within similar categories. For instance, knowing that you are teaching in a university classified in a certain way provides little information to help you understand the institutional framework of your course. Most colleges and universities today have produced mission statements and written documentation on the history and mission of the institution. Read them carefully. But official documents and a school's reputation merely approximate the lived experience of students and faculty. As the story about the basic course at one university suggests, many aspects of the course you will be teaching may be tied to unwritten portions of history and particular interpretations of the mission statement. The course director, department chair, and other faculty members should be able to provide you with a fuller sense of institutional history and how the mission is being implemented.

Consciously contextualize the course within the mission, history, and life of the institution in which you serve—when you get to the point of teaching the course, members of the community should recognize its fit. By no means does a proper fit suggest that every instructor's course should be identical to other sections of the course, past or present. To the contrary, you will bring a unique perspective and personal approach to the course. Also, institutional cultures and communities are dynamic places. Simply remember that no public speaking course belongs to you alone. You have primary responsibility for instruction and a well-defined role as the classroom instructor, but avoid the error of proceeding as though the course was yours alone.

If you are attentive to them, your students will instruct you quickly enough about the fact that every public speaking course is a collaborative, community experience.  They will bring their own perspectives on the institution, its mission, and campus life.  If possible, talk to a number of colleagues to begin to get a sense for student expectations of the public speaking course.  In larger universities, bookstores often carry fall guidebooks for freshmen, which rate the difficulty and common workload for required courses.  Although accuracy of such reports varies, you should be familiar with how the course is perceived by the student culture.  On smaller campuses, you will probably have to rely on casual conversations with students. Do not be surprised by what you may discover.  For instance, public speaking courses have a reputation for being contributors to grade inflation—an easy "A." In some cases freshmen dominate the course, which is oriented to introduce them to college-level studies, while in others students put off taking the course until the latest possible term before graduation.  The workload expected in the course varies widely as do the actual number of speeches.  You may choose to accentuate the positive attributes and ameliorate the negatives, but you need a sense for what students expect when they walk into your classroom.

The importance of recognizing the interdependence of the public speaking course with the institution at large can be seen through an example of what can happen when we neglect such a perspective. A liberal arts college with some strong professional programs once required all students to take a public speaking course.  A member of the faculty from another department in the college explained that the course was so weak and the instruction was so poor that the faculty decided to eliminate the course entirely and added public speaking requirements across the rest of the curriculum instead.  In other words, public speaking teachers lost a sense for the importance and connection of the course to the college and provided substandard instruction.  Students now receive no grounding in the art of public speaking; they merely receive occasional opportunities to practice without the necessary instruction or training. There were certainly other factors—academic and political—that contributed to the demise of the public speaking course at the institution. But the example is not isolated; many courses that should be required but lose their sense of connection to the life of the larger institution suffer such fates. Therefore, make it your business to get a comprehensive profile on the school from a variety perspectives and get a head start on how various constituencies served by the course perceive the public speaking course.

## Department: Linking the Institution and the Discipline

Most frequently, public speaking courses are offered through the communication or speech communication department. The department—your home as a teacher—mediates between the institution, with which you should now be somewhat familiar, and the scholarly discipline of communication. Give students a sense of how the course and your department fit within both realms. The department bridges two important intellectual communities of which you are a de facto member: the institutional community and the community of communication scholars. You live and work in both of them, a fact that should become evident to your students. Your classroom may be the first exposure that students have to someone working in the field of communication as a scholar and practitioner. The course will not only influence their perceptions of what it takes to speak effectively in public, but will also give them a distinct impression about what sort of questions interest people who study communication and how they address such questions. The quality of your instruction and the dynamism of your classroom as a learning environment should connect you to the discipline and your present and future work as a communication scholar. Expect interesting questions about communication to emerge from within the community of your institution and particularly through interaction with your students in the learning process.

## *Discipline: Yesterday, Today, and Tomorrow*

You have a unique opportunity to initiate your students into the field of communication through the public speaking course. On some occasions, instructors attempt to use the public speaking course as a promotional opportunity for the discipline by devoting a class session or two to talking about the communication field. We should recognize our promotional opportunities. but public speaking class does not lend itself well to surveying the possibilities for students within the field of communication. Neither does the course seem well suited to become a forum in which entire class sessions are dedicated to recruiting majors or minors for the department. However, as we have noted earlier, public speaking does play a foundational role in the history of the discipline, present thought and practice, and considerations for the future of communication.

Students should leave the course with a well-developed awareness of the role of public speaking in their society and with some sense of how they can use their skills and knowledge together to contribute to their communities today and tomorrow. Help them get situated historically, understanding how and why the course is being taught from a disciplinary perspective as well as from the perspective of the institution. For example, students will be glad to hear occasionally about exercises and assignments from the past through which they no longer are forced to suffer. They will also appreciate your clear explanations for the conceptual and skill demands currently being placed upon them—especially the connections you can make for them to their anticipated worlds beyond college. If you can make these connections, students will begin to grasp the pertinence of communication study to the world today and to the future.

Through the term, weave into the course your most interesting communication questions that have clear connections to various aspects of public speaking. For example, "How does a speaker call a particular audience into existence?" or, "To what degree does the audience participate in the creation of the message?" When you raise theoretical issues close to your own interests, you will naturally demonstrate genuine enthusiasm for the discipline. Looking for such connections should energize your classroom manner as well, giving students a much better sense for the intellectual attraction and demands of the communication field than any dry rehearsal of hypothetical applications of communication could possibly do for them.

## Mission and Objectives of Your Course

How would you answer a student who asked, "Why should I take your public speaking course?" You should have a succinct response and rationale in your own mind that any student could understand. The answer should concentrate first on the basic concepts and skills you want each student to master within the framework of your institution, department, and the discipline. Although you should present the mission and objectives of the course to a student in the order listed above, the development should probably begin with the department and move to concepts and skills.

## *Connection to Departmental Mission*

The course you teach should be purposely linked to the mission of your department.  As noted earlier, the department integrates the field of communication into the institutional community of your college or university.  The mission and objectives of the course should be clearly connected to both. Review the recurring emphases and themes in your own department.  Whether or not the department has formalized a mission statement, how would you state the departmental mission in your own words?  How does the course fit into the mission of the department?  Think about questions like these: How many students take the course in a given semester or in the school year?  Are Communication majors required to take public speaking?  What range of people teaches public speaking for the department?  What relationship, if any, exists between the course and funding for graduate students?  Does a faculty member direct the course?  If so, how much divergence exists between different sections of the course?  If not, what kind of direction comes from the department on teaching the course?  As you begin to fashion your approach to the course, a course calendar, assignments, and policies, make sure that they complement the larger mission of the department.

## *Specific Course Mission*

The official course description is a good place from which to launch your version of the public speaking course. How does the catalog of courses describe public speaking? Notice the similarities and differences in emphasis and specificity in the following course descriptions for public speaking courses. The selections come from institutions that vary widely in size, mission, location, etc. (Course numbers and other school-specific requirements have been omitted.  All information came from Internet sites, which can

be accessed on the NCA home page list of Communication Departments).

- *Public Presentations: Theory and Practice.* Basic elements of the theory and method of effective and responsible public address; practice in a variety of speech situations; relevant technology; analysis and criticism. BRADLEY UNIVERSITY

- *Essentials of Public Speaking.* Composition and delivery of speeches to inform and persuade. Logical organization is stressed. CALIFORNIA STATE UNIVERSITY—LONG BEACH

- *Public Speaking.* [Public Speaking] is a course that provides you the opportunity to improve your skills in public speaking.  In our global society, finding one's "voice" in issues relevant to local, national, and international issues requires both personal reflection and critical thought.  This course is designed to help hone those skills that can help you become a more informed, proficient, and well-spoken member of both academic and business communities.  COLORADO STATE UNIVERSITY

- *Public Speaking.* Practical and psychological principles of persuasive speech and negotiating. GENEVA COLLEGE

- *Public Speaking.* Develops communication skills necessary to analyze verbal discourse and to perform effectively in public speaking situations that confront the educated person. DUQUESNE UNIVERSITY

- *Public Communication.* Study and practice of the basic techniques of public speaking used to inform and persuade audiences. Emphasis on the speech-building process: research, composition, organization, style, delivery, and criticism. GEORGE WASHINGTON UNIVERSITY

- *Public Presentations.* This course introduces students to the theory and practice of public speaking. Topics covered include methods of organizing a speech and delivery, the types and uses of evidence, and the effective use of visual aids. Students prepare and deliver several speeches including an informative speech, a persuasive speech and occasional speech, and a career simulation. HOPE COLLEGE

- *Speaker-Audience Communication.* Study of rhetorical theory and its application to the preparation, presentation, and criticism of oral discourse in audience situations. Special consideration of listening behavior and of the ethical conduct of speech in a free society. This course fulfills the College oral communication requirement.  KANSAS UNIVERSITY

- *Public Speaking.* An advanced course in communication principles to develop skills in the analysis and presentation of speeches. MANKATO STATE UNIVERSITY

♦ *Introduction to Public Speaking.* Preparation, presentation, and criticism of speeches. Emphasis on the development of public speaking techniques through constructive criticism.  UNIVERSITY OF MONTANA

♦ *Public Speaking.* Theory and extensive practice in various types of speaking.  UNIVERSITY OF NORTH CAROLINA-CHAPEL HILL

♦ *Effective Speech.* Introduction to speech communication: formal speaking, group discussion, analysis and evaluation of messages.   Principles of communication, implemented through presentation of speeches, with some attention to group discussion and message evaluation.   PENN STATE UNIVERSITY

♦ *Presentational Communication.*  This course develops students' ability to research complex issues, organize facts, develop proposals, and competently deliver formal presentations to audiences. Presentational Communication curriculum offers a blend of public speaking skills (analytical, theoretical, and practical) and audience analysis skills (socio-demographic and psychological) to improve the effectiveness of students' oral communication, critical thinking, and listening skills. UNIVERSITY OF PUGET SOUND

♦ *Public Speaking.* Study of the principles of public address to include the preparation and delivery of various types of speeches.  STETSON UNIVERSITY

♦ *Public Speaking.* Training in speeches of social and technical interest designed to teach students to develop and illustrate ideas and information and to inform, stimulate, and persuade their audiences. TEXAS A&M UNIVERSITY

Note that while all the courses listed above seem to assume a performance component in the course—

that students will actually present speeches in class—the pedagogical objectives for the courses differ.  The

specific mission of your course should provide more detail than a course catalog description.  It should

begin to answer the student question "Why take public speaking?" How much emphasis will be placed on

preparation, organization, delivery, listening, critical thinking, types of speeches, research, visual support

(conventional and electronic), theory, evidence, ethics, psychology, politics, business, academics, group

speaking? Your version of the course will not be able to include everything, so the mission should explain

the focus and provide some basic reasons for the direction to be taken in the course.

## *Basic Course Objectives*

To answer an inquiring student decisively, you need to outline objectives that make the mission of the course concrete. What are the principles, concepts, and skills that you expect students to learn? The list you state should be simple—not exhaustive, but 3-5 main objectives. Nevertheless, make them specific enough that at the end of the term, students can assess the course and your effectiveness at achieving the objectives. A careful inspection of the textbook might get you started in this process. But most textbooks are designed to support your work in the course—you will still need to be selective about how to use the textbook and other resources. Remember Carroll Arnold's simple set of objectives—at the conclusion of the course, public speaking students should be able to:

1.  Organize their messages.

2.  Adapt their messages to the audience.

3.  Speak extemporaneously.

The following examples show three variations on course missions and sets of objectives:

|  | **Course I** | **Course II** | **Course III** |
|---|---|---|---|
| **Mission** | To build competence at preparing and presenting speeches in a variety of workplace and community contexts. | To build competence in critical analysis and presentation of spoken public discourse. | To build presentational competence grounded in theoretical understanding of public speaking situations and practices. |
| **Objectives** | 1.  1. To organize a message. | 1.  To conduct critical analysis of public messages. | 1. To conceptualize the dynamics of speaking situations and practices. |
|  | 2.  To adapt a message to the audience. | 2.  To research a message. | 2.  To organize a message. |
|  | 3.  To speak individually and in group contexts. | 3.  To organize a message. | 3.  To adapt a message to the audience. |
|  | 4.  4. To speak extemporaneously. | 4.  To speak extemporaneously. | 4.  To speak extemporaneously. |

Given the status of your course within the larger mission of the department within your institution and the field of communication, write or record the mission of your course and a set of course objectives that answer the question "Why take public speaking?"

# Extemporaneous Speaking

As you probably noticed, every set of objectives in the preceding table includes "To speak extemporaneously." Each of the four Allyn & Bacon public speaking textbooks mentioned earlier focuses on extemporaneous delivery. Were you to survey every public speaking textbook published in the past 25 years, you would be hard-pressed to find one that encourages students to write a manuscript, to memorize their speech, or to speak impromptu. (Most make exceptions for impromptu speaking under circumstances that precludes adequate preparation.)

## *Predominance in public speaking courses*

Introductory courses in public speaking are dominated by the extemporaneous method of delivery. Although most textbooks explain four delivery alternatives—memorization, manuscript, impromptu, and extemporaneous—a quick review of their pages reveals that the methods taught deal almost exclusively with extemporaneous speaking. As David Zarefsky explains in his public speaking text,

Extemporaneous presentation . . . is generally recommended for most speakers and speeches, because it encourages a conversational quality and is flexible enough to permit adaptation. Extemporaneous speaking is not impromptu; the speaker has planned the speech carefully, has a specific structure in mind, and probably has outlined the speech and prepared notes for use during presentation. But it also is not memorized or manuscript; the word-for-word text does not exist in advance of the speaker's delivery. In other words, the speech is prepared and rehearsed, but it is neither written out nor memorized. (354)

Extemporaneous speaking has been practiced from earliest recorded history in the field. However, in many historical moments, students have been steered toward memorization of famous speeches or other literature, and experienced public speaking teachers continue to meet students who were taught to memorize or write manuscripts for their presentations in high school Speech or English courses. Nevertheless, we have geared the overwhelming majority of college public speaking courses toward extemporaneous speaking today and that almost exclusively. Why?

## *Rationale for Emphasis*

People in the general public still think about a speech as "written." Indeed, most of the political speeches, news coverage, and commentary seen and heard by the public on media outlets are variations on manuscript speaking. But public speaking pedagogy assumes that such presentations constitute a small fraction of all of the public speaking that goes on in the world on any given day. In other words, although people might expect that good speakers need to write out speeches word-for-word and either read the manuscript or memorize their remarks, public speaking pedagogy promotes extemporaneous delivery. The depth of commitment to extemporaneous speaking emerges from at least three commonplaces: (1) practical considerations; (2) theoretical commitments; (3) superior preparation for the whole range of speaking situations.

Most of the presentations most people give should be delivered extemporaneously. Through the course of their working lives and beyond, most students will need extemporaneous delivery skills much more than any other presentation method. The majority of workplace speaking situations are best suited to such presentations. But many presenters work without any grasp of extemporaneous delivery, use other methods, and communicate in a mediocre fashion (to which professionals have grown accustomed). If our students can learn strong extemporaneous speaking skills, then they stand to improve the communication in their workplaces and communities as well as advancing their ideas effectively.

Extemporaneous speaking rests on a solid conceptual base. Even if there were not such remarkable practical advantages to extemporaneous delivery, most communication scholars would advocate the method based on theoretical grounds, such as the transactional nature of human communication—the idea that human beings in face-to-face contact are simultaneously sending, interpreting, generating, and receiving messages. Therefore, speakers who can employ a delivery method that promotes full participation with the audience in a transactional mode are positioned to communicate most effectively. Speakers need to read and respond to audience feedback during the presentation. For a prepared message, only extemporaneous delivery allows for such interchanges with the audience.

Finally, extemporaneous speaking places a wider variety of demands on students, and prepares them to perform the other methods of delivery more effectively if necessary. Speakers accustomed to developing extemporaneous speeches are more likely to write manuscripts addressed to the ears of the audience— writing for the ear rather than the eye. Likewise, they will be less fearful about eye contact and the broad range of non-verbal communication at their disposal, recognizing the need for fuller communication with the audience, whether speaking from the pages of a manuscript or from memory. Extemporaneous speaking introduces students to the contrast between the spoken and written word and helps them to begin

to train themselves in oral practices and performance.

# Chapter Two:
# Preparing for the Term

Whether you are reading this training guide three months, three weeks, or three days prior to the start of the semester, you want to be well prepared to guide students through the learning experience we call public speaking. Concerning your own version of the course, you may be experiencing many of the same feelings that your students will before their speeches. The questions are relatively simple: What is my role as the instructor in this particular course? What text should I use and how can I use it most effectively? How should I structure the course? What about class policies? How do I build a good syllabus? You must work out the detailed answers to these questions, but the following discussion provides some starting points and coordinates to get prepared and frame the course to accomplish your instructional objectives.

## The Roles of the Instructor in the Course

You will wear many instructional hats while teaching public speaking—many more than in most courses. Negotiating your multiple roles as the classroom instructor will be a continuing process in public speaking. Your willingness and ability to do so may greatly enhance the learning experience for students. As mentioned earlier, in most public speaking courses the material to be covered in conventional classroom sessions is compressed into approximately one half of the class meetings to allow time for student speaking experiences. Of this limited time, students seem to benefit from various exercises and discussion, so while lectures might cover the material most efficiently, instructional effectiveness may suffer by making lectures the predominant instructional method. Your role as instructor during student performances also requires careful consideration and places you in another set of roles altogether.

## Instructor-Student Relationship as Predictor of Student Experience

Your classroom personality, presence, and practices will be the dominant factor in students' experience of the public speaking course. Based on my own interaction with many instructors, students, and course directors, the instructor seems to play the crucial role in whether or not students really attend to the material or simply go through the motions. *Because of their instructors,* many students come to enjoy the course despite the anxiety attached to giving speeches. On the other hand, some students who could learn the material and excel in performance suffer through the course *because of their instructors.* In many cases, difficulties can be attributed to personality conflicts. Personality matters in a course like public speaking. As a result, I regularly tell students that they should transfer to another section of the course or drop and take the course another semester from a different instructor if they feel uncomfortable with me personally or suspect we might have problems. But in most cases, preparation for the different roles required of you and identifying those roles for students in advance can make the learning experience positive for the great majority of students who come to your class.

## Demands of Instructing a Performance Course

You will be teaching a course in which a student could receive 100% of the points available on every written assignment including exams and only manage a *B* in the course. The course should be structured so that more points are dedicated to speeches than any other activity. Therefore, students who do not present their speeches effectively may receive lower grades than they are accustomed to in most academic subjects.  Such occurrences are rare.  But you will encounter highly literate students who believe that their conceptual mastery should translate into positive performance evaluations, even though their speeches are mediocre.  You will also have students who genuinely worked tirelessly for hours on a five-minute speech that completely flops.  They may expect a higher mark based on their effort.  Students want classes to prepare them for the "real world," but not like you will prepare them.  The real world is a place where performance counts—where clients or bosses or customers or constituents never see the preparation, only the actual performance—and people make judgments on the quality of the presentation alone.  They must, and so must you.

Students may believe that you ask them to do too much and then grade them too subjectively.  Because the course demands that they develop new cognitive skills and communication practices, they *should* feel like you are asking them to do too much at once.  Although you will have a grading system that focuses on objectively observable behaviors and components in their speeches, they may initially have the sense that you are grading them in a subjective, arbitrary manner—especially if they believe they deserve a higher grade than they receive.  The fact of performance and the evaluation of performance put you in a different situation than courses with no performance component, and these aspects permeate the entire course.  But the course also places unique performance demands on you as the instructor that students will recognize almost immediately and that need to be managed with poise and agility.

## Dynamics of Dual Roles: Instructor and Performer

As you have probably anticipated, your role as a performer in the classroom will be accentuated. Public speaking teachers have to practice what we preach.  Composition teachers need not ever submit their own writing to student scrutiny, but students will immediately get a sense for your speaking skills. If you have extensive speaking experience, the performance factor should be relatively comfortable and your thoughts may turn to how you can utilize your own experience most effectively in the classroom context. However, if you possess only limited speaking experience or are being asked to teach the course having never been trained in public speaking through a college course or professional seminar, the prospect can be intimidating. Later we will deal with modeling presentation skills in class more specifically. For now, recognize that you need not be an accomplished presenter to teach this course well. Use the course to learn and practice in advance the skills for which you will hold your students accountable when they speak. The performance skills you consciously hone in public speaking can be usefully transferred to every other course you teach. Many aspects of effective pedagogical communication parallel the ideas and skills you will teach in public speaking, so concentrate on improving your own performances in class. You will benefit yourself and your students.

## *Dynamics of Dual Roles: Coach and Judge*

A most difficult dilemma arises when you must grade the performance of students whom you have taught. The course calls on you to play the dual roles of coach and judge. For example, an Olympic ice skating coach invests hours of teaching in the performance of an athlete. Then, when the competition begins, the coach helps prepare and encourage the skater to handle the situation and deliver a peak performance. Someone else judges the performance. As a public speaking instructor, like a coach or trainer, you will teach students the concepts and skills expected to be enacted in their speeches. You will want them to do well. However, just when your students are ready to "step onto the ice," you will have to take to the judges' stand and evaluate their performances as impartially as possible.

Many instructors struggle with this paradox. The difficulties associated with the dual role of coach and judge surround three main issues: (1) How do performances reflect teaching effectiveness? (2) How will this grade affect future performances? (3) How will the student respond to me as a teacher if I give this grade? None of these questions has an easy answer, but in each case new instructors are susceptible to contributing to grade inflation by following the path of least resistance. Let me explain.

First, do not use student performances—strong or weak—as a gauge of instructional effectiveness. A novice's performance cannot be reduced to instruction alone. Apprehension (especially in early speaking rounds), inadequate preparation, romance lost or found, an exam in another class the same day, or any number of other factors may contribute to a poor performance. Therefore, your evaluation should not be tempered in favor of the student because they did not execute what you taught. To do so assumes a pedagogical failure. Your evaluation scheme should reflect the concepts and skills you have emphasized in class. Explain the evaluation form clearly and indicate the standards for grade ranges in advance. Over the entire course, your teaching will play a significant role in student development. But the connections between teaching and particular performances are varied, indirect, and quite dependent on each student's particular level of engagement in the course. If you see a pattern in which the majority of students omit something you thought you had taught clearly, maintain the same standard throughout the speaking round and make adjustments before the next set of speeches.

Second, vow to yourself never to use a grade as a motivation tool, positively or negatively. Some teachers purposely grade the first round of speeches low—no one gets above a B. These instructors believe that their students rise to the challenge and make greater improvement through the term if their first performance is judged harshly. Most new instructors take the opposite tack. They fear that students will be discouraged by a low grade. In these cases, an *F* becomes a *C*, a *D* becomes a *B*, a *C* becomes an *A-*, a *B* becomes an *A*, and an *A* becomes an *A+*. Use your written comments and suggestions as motivators, not grades. Practice saying, "you got a high mark on this speech, but you have a number of ways to improve," and "your evaluation was low because of these factors in the speech, but you can address them by . . ." Instructors have neither the power to degrade nor to elevate anyone's self-esteem through a single speech grade. But you can mislead, which could give a student an inaccurate impression about their level of performance that could harm them in the future.

Third, resist the temptation to curry favor or "buy" good teaching evaluations with speech grades. Beginning teachers commonly succumb to the desire to be well received/liked by their students. Giving slightly higher grades where possible seems to be a good way to win favor. The reasoning on teaching evaluations follows a simple syllogistic pattern: teaching evaluations correlate directly with expected grades in the course (the higher the grades, the higher the teaching evaluations); I will make sure that everyone who comes to class and tries in this course receives an *A* or a *B*; I will receive favorable teaching evaluations. The syllogism breaks down in the initial premise. The correlation between grades and teaching evaluation is a contested question. Furthermore, reflect on your best, most highly respected teachers. Do you rate them primarily based on the grades you earned in their class?

In summary, you need to prepare yourself and your students for the different roles you will need to play through the term, especially the ones associated with performance aspects of the course. Articulate the roles that you are playing as the course develops. Doing so will enable students to adjust their expectations and will help them maximize their learning experience with you. Recognize the impact of your classroom presence on the quality of student experiences in the course overall, own your responsibility to practice what you preach in class, and make the distinctions between your dual roles as coach and judge clear, without compromising either one.

# Choosing a Text and Supplements

You experienced a variety of uses for textbooks in your college career (some of which had no connection to the course you were taking). Try to remember cases in which a textbook that enhanced your learning experience was neglected by your professor. There may be a few. But in most cases, the effectiveness of the textbook can be linked to the instructor's active use of the text in the class. How do you expect students to use the book? Will you expect them to bring their books to each class meeting? If you ask them to, will they continue to do so because of your regular use of the text as a learning tool? What can you do to help students to utilize the book seriously, not just read it the night before a test?

## *The Role of the Text in the Course*

When you begin to teach public speaking, the textbook will be one of the most important components in your regimen. You know why the textbook is important to you. One of your main tasks is deciding how the textbook will become important to your students. As you know, college instructors tend not to cover the text in detail during class sessions. First, most college instructors design a course to reflect their personal knowledge and experience in the subject. Second, between their own knowledge, the text, other material, and the time constraints of the course, no one could cover the territory comprehensively in class alone. Finally, college courses include the expectation that students gain much of their knowledge outside of class time. While this should make the text more important to students, they will not take the text seriously unless you do. No one but you can define the role of the text in your class. Students will value the text depending upon your expectations for them to rely on the text in class sessions, assignments, and exams.

Following are some ideas about roles that the text can play in a student's learning experience. I suggest that you try them all initially, discarding only those which seem to you to be fruitless after three or more semesters.

## Pre-class Preparation

Students will learn more if they come to class with their mental pumps primed by a first encounter with the material in the textbook. Some instructors quiz regularly to keep students up to speed. Others assign one or two discussion questions to be submitted for minimal credit (perhaps "participation") for each reading assignment. The latter approach seems superior in the sense that the discussion can be incorporated into the class session, thereby encouraging students to integrate their reading with the material introduced in class. Quizzes tend to get students focused on the text as a source of points, which the student mind unreflectively stores in short-term memory (a.k.a., not to be learned). Discussion questions collected at the beginning of the class are one way to get students to read without nagging them.

## Source of Activities and Exercises

If students work with the textbook in class they will value it more and learn more from it outside of class. Quality textbooks incorporate a variety of activities and exercises from which to select. You should receive a desk copy with special notes for instructors and an instructor's manual that includes additional activities, exercises, and assignments. Choose activities from the text that effectively reinforce class concepts. Many texts also include "special feature" segments within the regular text that highlight their emphases—these too can be used as discussion points.

## Examples

From antiquity, public speaking teachers have recognized that models help students learn the concepts and strategies necessary to excel. Because speaking is a performance, examples of the concepts and skills taught in the course are particularly helpful and plentiful. Textbooks broaden the scope of examples. Most include a variety of student speeches and noteworthy public speeches; some publishers also provide videotapes of both kinds of speech. No student will connect with every example in class or in the book, so a wide assortment serves to enhance learning opportunities. Examples can be used for discussion and as case studies.

## Reference

Student appreciation for the textbook may grow as their graded speech assignments approach. What initially may seem dry and difficult reading can come to life as they are planning their own speech. Give them reminders. In your written evaluations, prescribe particular sections of the text, even specific pages, to help them improve on the weaknesses you diagnose in their early speeches.

In the public speaking course, you will be the most important source of information and direction for your students, but a well-employed textbook can enhance student learning by supplementing and reinforcing the objectives and content of your course.

## *If You Select the Text: Factors to Consider*

The department or the course director often selects the text with which new public speaking teachers begin. However, today or at some future time you may have to select your own textbook for the course. First recognize that a variety of fine textbooks are available. To make a good selection for your course, *review the mission of the university, department, and course.* A number of textbooks will probably fit. Next, *review your objectives for the course.* At this point, certain texts should begin to distinguish themselves as more appropriate for your situation. For example, while almost all public speaking texts today reflect sensitivity to critical thinking and reasoning, speaker apprehension, diversity issues, and speaking in the workplace, the Allyn & Bacon public speaking texts noted earlier place particular emphasis on each of these themes respectively.

If your course mission and objectives emphasize critical thinking and reasoning, then *Public Speaking: Strategies for Success,* by David Zarefsky would complement the course. Almost every public speaking text includes a few tips on dealing with the stage fright so commonly experienced by speakers. But *Mastering Public Speaking,* by George L. Grice & John F. Skinner, devotes an entire chapter to the subject. Textbooks reflect the current emphasis on diversity in a variety of ways, but some instructors have chosen to build their entire course around this popular theme. For such versions of the course, *Public Speaking in the Age of Diversity,* by Teri Kwal Gamble & Michael W. Gamble, thoroughly integrates public speaking and diversity. *Public Speaking: An Audience-Centered Approach,* by Steven A. Beebe & Susan J. Beebe foregrounds audience issues throughout and keeps readers focused on the connections between the public speaking classroom and workplace presentations which students can anticipate.

To decide between comparable texts that complement your mission and objectives in the course, consider the students who will be taking the class. While texts may fit equally well, they differ in reading difficulty.   Among otherwise comparable books, the organization of one may suit the length and structure

of your term better than another.  A book that works well during a semester may present more difficulties

when adapted to a quarter system or an accelerated summer term.  Also, a book with examples geared

toward traditional freshmen may not be adequate to meet the needs of a class populated by non-traditional

students.

Finally, the book should be one that complements your own teaching commitments, pedagogical

style, and strengths as an instructor.  The presentation of concepts, examples, and activities need to resonate

well with you for the text to enhance the course in a meaningful way.  If you cannot connect with the

textbook, students will probably resent being expected to buy it in the first place, because you will not be

inclined to incorporate it meaningfully into class sessions.

## Supplementing the Text

As you approach the first round of student speeches, you may want to show a sample student

speech—an example of a peer performing well.  Perhaps you want to inspire your students by exposing

them to an exemplary speech by a popular figure.  Maybe students would benefit from some software aids

regarding speech design or effective use of the Internet.  All of these cases can be addressed by using

resources you select to supplement the text.  You might be able to find supplements like the ones

mentioned above by searching yourself, but most quality textbooks today include a wide range of

supplemental materials designed to complement your textbook selection.  Many of these items are provided

for you at no charge; others are available for a modest fee.  For students, you may elect to include speech

design software, speech planning workbooks, Internet use for speech research guides, etc.  Allyn & Bacon

publishers provide a complete spectrum of supplements for teachers and students.  In the final chapter of this training manual you will find a matrix connecting these supplements with the appropriate chapters of Allyn & Bacon's public speaking textbooks.

You may also choose to supplement the textbook with a variety of handouts, including speech texts from the past (recent and distant) or worksheets of your own design. Providing working handouts which encourage students to develop their speech ideas as you proceed through the conceptual material in the course will help them to stay engaged with the material you are teaching. I personally recommend that you select or develop a speech evaluation form and attempt to plan your major assignments in advance with assignment sheets for students. If you can combine your handouts, assignment sheets, and evaluation forms into a packet that can be purchased inexpensively at the campus bookstore(s), you will provide a valuable supplemental resource for your students and save yourself much time and energy at the copy machine during the term.

## Structuring the Course

You have the foundation set for your course. You should possess a sense of how your version of public speaking fits in your community. Your teaching objectives are set and you have selected a textbook that resonates with your general instructional plan. Now you must establish a structure to make your version of the course a concrete learning experience for you and your students. Use the syllabus as a tool to develop that structure. If you are working within a standard syllabus for the course, review the syllabus and master these elements *before* the course begins, reflecting on how you will implement them in your particular classroom.

## *Strategic Development of the Syllabus*

Think of your syllabus as a blueprint or owner's manual for the course.  No one should be forced to read one in its entirety (many students do not anyway), but each of the particulars may become crucial to the effectiveness of a larger project in its own time.  As the person in charge of running the course, you should always be able to see the whole in relationship to each part.  As you develop or work through the syllabus, make sure that the agenda it sets reflects your expectations for students and your commitments to the course.  The syllabus also should be a realistic rendering of the possible regarding instruction.  Likewise, the policies contained in it should be enforceable and aimed at enhancing performance rather than entrapment and retribution.

## *Number of Class Sessions in the Term*

The first reality check of your instructional aspirations should come as you reflect on the number and length of the class sessions in the term.  Face the fact that, whether you are teaching a semester, quarter, summer term, degree-completion program, or any other format, you simply will not have enough time.  Once you have adjusted to the fundamental limitation of time, the configuration of your term still makes a significant difference.  Regardless of the type of term, you still must provide students with instruction and performance opportunities.  But how you do this and how the term structure affects student learning will vary widely.  Will your students be taking four to five other courses simultaneously?  How close will their first, second, and third speeches be to one another in time?  Will a speaking round last two weeks or two days?  Will a speaking round last two class sessions or six?  How will you divide instructional time?  You should address these issues and factors as you prepare your course calendar.  Expect the process of developing the calendar to involve a good deal of juggling and compromise before you arrive at a workable arrangement.

## *Framework of Instruction, Speeches, and Evaluation*

Public speaking teachers must make compromises in developing a course calendar because approximately one half of class sessions are ordinarily devoted to graded student speech performances. You may include other, non-graded speaking exercises or activities as well. Therefore, instructional time is precious. The performance aspect of the course puts pressure on all of the remaining class sessions.

The syllabus frames the role of instruction, speech performances, and evaluation via speech grading and exams. I understand that some instructors choose to divide the term in half, front-loading all of the traditional classroom instruction in the first half of the term and then using the second half of the term for student speeches. Ordinarily, teachers choose to take a more incremental approach, introducing basic skills and working up to the more sophisticated aspects of speech design, reasoning, argumentation, and presentation as the term progresses. Therefore, if you are building your own syllabus, you need to make choices about what to include and where in the course to insert each instructional segment you choose.

For example, how many speeches and of what type will you require? Will you include some instruction on ceremonial speaking and on serving as a master of ceremonies? Read ahead to the section on speaking rounds. How much time will you allot for each student's speech, including time you allow for peer feedback and your comments? Will you include a visit to the campus library? Do you expect to incorporate instruction on group presentations? Perhaps you want to show videos of student speeches and famous speakers. How many class sessions will that require? Will you devote time to impromptu speaking? You will also need to decide how many exams or quizzes to include.

Finally, consider how your course fits with the rest of your responsibilities—other courses you may be teaching or taking, other employment. or personal plans and commitments. Remember that whatever you assign must also be graded. so consider how much time the course will require. For instance, if you have not graded speeches before you should probably allow about 15-20 minutes per speech.

## Course Policies

Establish your expectations for key elements and processes in the course in the syllabus. A special section devoted to "course policies" can help you to avoid difficulties during the term. In public speaking classes, attendance. grading, cheating, and access to the instructor are all major factors to consider. You may have other policies or issues within your particular course. Setting the parameters and policies must come at the beginning of the term. Students rarely respond favorably to mid-course changes or late introduction of policies.

## Attendance

Full participation by all students in every class session makes a big difference in the vitality and quality of the learning process in public speaking. Make attendance mandatory unless you can come up with strong rationale for letting students come and go as they please. Why? Without the mandate, certain students will routinely miss the learning opportunities available during speaking rounds because "they're only giving speeches today." Some of the most important learning that can possibly take place in a public speaking course should be happening during student speeches. But absences. particularly by students who have already presented their speeches, can seriously detract from the classroom environment for other speakers and generally sap the energy from the course.

Some instructors make attendance mandatory, but tell students that they may miss two to three class sessions without penalty. Acknowledging to yourself that students may not be able to make each and every class meeting is realistic; however, I recommend that the grace applied to the first few absences not be announced publicly but merely applied at the end of the course. If you allow for two or three "personal days," then students will use them and may expect more leniency in general. Expect your students to communicate with you every time they miss class. Do not count legitimate absences, but do penalize frivolous ones. Using language such as, "you should *expect* absences to have a negative impact on your grade," gives you flexibility to apply the attendance policy fairly, but sends the message that students should be in every class possible.

## Grading System

To call grades a preoccupation with students severely understates the case. At some point in the term, most students are likely to review this segment of the syllabus to check their status in the course. Your grading scale, the values assigned to each assignment, and how you handle late work, extra credit, and complaints will all be scrutinized by a number of your students each term. Therefore, think through each of these areas and any other grade-related issues presented by your course.

Most colleges and universities use a standard grading scale. If one exists, use it. If not, determine the predominant grading scale that students encounter and incorporate it if possible.

The values you assign to each assignment—how you balance speeches, exams, exercises, etc., will be more important than the grading scale you list. First, give priority to assigning the largest proportion of points to speeches. In certain exceptional cases, an instructor might justify assigning a larger proportion of

credit to other elements of the course than to the total amount of points available for speeches. However,

speeches should ordinarily make up at least 40 percent of the total points and, when combined with specific

speech preparation and evaluation, assignments might reach 60 to 70 percent of credit for the course.

Second, do not cave in to the feeling some instructors get that students will only do assignments worth

points. Save your points for substantial exercises, exams, papers, and speeches. If you want students to do

class preparation work for which they receive no credit, provide the rationale for the work. Find ways to

reward people who participate, like including the work in examination material or providing helpful

feedback on the assignment only to participants. I recommend that you stick to a 1,000-point scale and

break your evaluations into five-point increments whenever possible, especially on exams. Make test items

worth at least five points and then use factors of five. By doing so, you make clear distinctions between

grades, resist the temptation in yourself to award discretionary points, and suppress the inclination of some

students to argue over a single point.

On speech grades specifically, two options are popular. You can value each speech equally,

assuming that skill development is incremental. The first speech is worth as much as the last (or roughly

so) because a great deal had to be learned to accomplish the first, whereas every speech afterward takes the

earlier learning for granted. The value is assigned according to the additional skills and concepts attending

the later speeches. On the other hand, you can create an ascending point value for each speech, assuming

that students should be given time to develop and mature as speakers. The first evaluated speech should be

"safe" so that doing poorly as an inexperienced speaker does not disqualify students from achieving high

marks for the course. Either choice can work effectively, depending on how the instructor handles each one. In general, the former encourages students to take the early speeches more seriously, and the latter tends to be more conducive to grade inflation.

In addition to these grading basics, your syllabus should reflect your policies on late work and extra credit. When is work considered "late"? *If I ask for an extension, should I expect a point deduction, or does my request negate any penalty?* I recommend that you establish a standard, workable policy for late work. Some instructors use a scale of diminishing points depending on how late the work is submitted. Others establish a standard percentage deduction. For speeches, you need to consider whether you will permit students to make up speeches that they skip and, if so, what penalty you will apply to a late speech. You should also set the process for making up speeches in advance, and make-ups should never compromise the quality of the learning/instructional experience for students who are prepared to speak on time.

What about extra credit? *If I discover I am doing poorly at the end of your course, can I get a personal assignment of extra work to make up the difference and keep my grade point average up?* In many cases, colleagues or graduate students will want you to offer extra credit as an incentive for students to participate as research subjects. Will all students be permitted to participate? If not, what alternative extra credit options will you provide for those not selected for a study or who cannot participate due to other constraints? *How much extra credit could I possibly get as a student? If I end the course with a 70 percent based on the merits of the regular work, how high can my grade ascend?* I recommend that you not allow extra credit to move any student more than four percent above the level they earn through the usual work in public speaking. Students can move from a low grade in a range to a higher version of the same grade, or they can move from the top of one range to the bottom of another, but no more than that.

Finally, a syllabus that outlines a process for managing grade complaints in public speaking will protect you from frivolous grade complaints and end of the semester "I need to get the _____ to: get into this major or social organization; keep my scholarship; remain eligible." A good grade complaint policy should include at least the following elements:

1.  *Do not discuss a grade immediately after the student receives it.* Require the students to take time (at least 24 hours) to reflect on their performance and your evaluation, not just react to the disjunction between their grades and their expectations.

2.  *Do not discuss grades in the classroom or in the hall.* Reserve such discussions for appointments. By doing so you protect the student's confidentiality and avoid the expansion of the personal matter to the class as a whole. A grade is only the business of the instructor and the concerned student.

3.  *Establish a statute of limitations (one-to-two weeks) after which assignment grades (speeches, exams, papers, etc.) will not be reviewed.* If a student is concerned about a grade on its own merits rather than how it detracts from the desired GPA, then she or he will make a point of speaking with you about it soon after the grade is assigned. Otherwise, disappointed students tend to choose grades on which they believe they can make the best case, not because they objected originally, but because as the consequences of their performance begin to materialize they want points to improve their grades at the last minute.

4.  *Demand that all evaluated materials be brought to a grade appeal meeting.* Documentation helps you and the student. You need to review the bases on which you assigned the grade. Also, you could be mistaken, whether mathematically or in the substance of your evaluation. But you have to be able to see it to make that assessment.

5.   *Require that the grade appeal be put in writing.* This benefits the student as well as you. First, the work involved in writing the appeal discourages complaints without merit. Second, the written appeal allows the student to think through her/his case and present it clearly, which can be difficult to do when attempting to launch the appeal in a one-on-one conversation. Finally, you get an opportunity to hear the complaint as a whole. The written complaint limits the scope of the discussion and can help to bring it to a satisfactory resolution more swiftly.

While the above suggestions are applicable to a variety of courses, they are especially pertinent to public speaking. Instructors and students alike understand the necessarily subjective aspects of evaluating speech performances. Clarifying your grade appeal process makes grade complaints a much more serious matter for students, deflecting frivolous complaints and averting personal embarrassment for some. By taking the initiative, you redirect the purpose of reviewing student concerns and put yourself in the position to either retain or revise your initial judgment, but to maintain a high level of respect with the student, regardless. As a good friend of mine was fond of saying to students, "I spent 30 minutes listening to and evaluating your speech. I expect the same kind of investment from you if you want me to reconsider. Surely, you don't think I'd forsake all that work and overturn it in a moment without full documentation and a careful review!"

## Academic Integrity

In most institutions, public speaking presents special challenges in the area of academic integrity. Many sections of the course are offered each semester, which means that material from the course is widely available. Students find the prospect of giving a speech nerve-wracking, and so may be more severely tempted to violate ethical standards in the process of getting help. Stories are legion of speech files maintained by fraternities, sororities, and other social organizations to save time and produce grades for

members. More recently, Internet sites reportedly provide "canned" speeches on assorted topics to help

students cut corners and meet standards. Less legendary, but perhaps more common are groups of students

taking the course in different sections during the same term trying to economize on labor by collaborating

on research, organization, visual aids, and more.

First, familiarize yourself with the stated policy of your college or university on academic integrity.

Your syllabus should identify the course with these standards. Then you must define what the general

standards mean in your version of the public speaking course. What constitutes plagiarism in a speech?

Can students work together on any aspect of research or speech design? Can previous work be used in your

class? While you are reviewing the institutional policies and definitions, review the procedure you should

follow if you suspect an infraction against academic integrity. If someone is cheating in your class, you

want to know the first move and what sorts of options you possess.

The most important decision to consider is how you will orient yourself and the course toward the

possibility for infractions, which occur every term in at least some sections of the course. Obviously, you

could simply choose to devote no attention to the reality of cheating and other violations in your class. Few

instructors exercise this option. Practically, you have two clear emphases from which to choose: either

structure the course assignments to make cheating difficult and unlikely to produce the desired result (a

better grade) or structure the course to enable you to identify and document instances of cheating easily.

Please consider where you want to expend your primary instructional energy and proceed accordingly.

In either case, students should know your definitions and expectations regarding academic integrity

by reading your course policies. Picture yourself reviewing the policy with someone who has committed an

infraction. They should be feeling intensely foolish, with no way to weasel out, whether they collaborated, plagiarized, or violated the policy in some other way. Also, make sure that you refer to the policies and give examples in class the first day and at other appropriate times through the semester. Note in your grade book and lesson plans the class sessions in which you spoke about academic integrity.

You must note the times you speak about academic integrity in class along with stating your policy in the syllabus to document that you do, in fact, take academic integrity seriously. Some students will claim that they did not understand the policy and could not have been expected to because of instructor negligence. Follow the process outlined in your school's code of ethics, student handbook, or the equivalent. Every time you meet with a student about possible infractions, document the meeting and its outcome. If the decisions you make are ever appealed or challenged, you will be glad for the paper trail.

In most institutions, you will determine the penalty for violations of academic integrity. Seek to avoid playing the merciless savior of the corrupted academy. On the other hand, the process of prosecution for cheating or other violation is not, in itself, a sufficient consequence. The second chance most students need comes by assisting them in negotiating the severe difficulties that should attend cheating, not in premature absolution.

## Accessibility

Think about the times and places students are most likely to be able to meet with you. Then review your own schedule to determine your time commitments and how your free moments match up with opportunities to meet with students. If you can, find times when your students can meet with you conveniently and in which you are unlikely to be able to get much work done anyway. In some cases, you may choose to meet students for office hours in a context other than your office. For example, you might find a quiet spot in a coffee shop or other comfortable meeting place on campus. Also, determine how you will make yourself accessible to students via telephone and e-mail.  Make your availability clear to them; follow through on your commitments.

## *Finalizing the Syllabus*

At this point you have thought through everything from your role as an instructor to determining when and how students can contact you outside of class.  If you use the elements of the syllabus to guide your planning and the structure for the course, when it comes to writing the syllabus you will have only to plug in the various components.  Complete the syllabus segments in reverse order, as follows.

Set your course calendar and include reading selection and major assignment due dates.  Students may not refer to the calendar frequently, but when they do, they will know what is happening.  As you determine how to incorporate the major assignments, write a brief description of each assignment and your exam format(s). Next, formalize your course policies in writing, explaining attendance and participation expectations, grading, and academic integrity issues.

The last two components to finalize should be your statement on why students should take public speaking and your objectives, plus any instructions students will need to contact you.  Therefore, when you finish the syllabus, it should proceed from contact information, to objectives, through course policies and major assignments, which finally take shape in the concrete dates and assignments in the course calendar.

Many challenges and opportunities will arise impromptu during the term—things that we can never account for in a syllabus.  However, the process of working through the issues, challenges, and opportunities necessary to build a solid syllabus will put you in the best position to negotiate the unanticipated to the best advantage of the learning process for you and your public speaking students.

# Chapter Three:
# Putting the Plan into Action

You have framed your version of public speaking. Now you must prepare to take it into the

classroom. It is a situation not unlike the beginning of *The Voyage of the Dawn Treader*; the third book in

C.S. Lewis' children's series, *The Chronicles of Narnia*. The scene opens while a sister and brother, Lucy

and Edmund Pevensie are remembering their previous adventures in Narnia.

The story begins on an afternoon when Edmund and Lucy were stealing a few precious minutes

alone together. And of course they were talking about Narnia, which was the name of their own

private and secret country. Most of us, I suppose, have a secret country but for us it is only an

imaginary country. Edmund and Lucy were luckier than other people in that respect. Their secret

country was real. They had already visited it twice; not in a game or a dream, but in reality. They

had got there of course by magic, which is the only way of getting into Narnia. And a promise, or

very nearly a promise, had been made them in Narnia itself that they would some day get back.

You may imagine that they talked about it a good deal, when they got the chance.

They were in Lucy's room, sitting on the edge of her bed and looking at a picture on the

opposite wall. It was the only picture in the house that they liked. Aunt Alberta didn't like it at all

(that was why it was put away in a little back room upstairs), but she couldn't get rid of it because it

had been a wedding present from someone she did not want to offend.

It was a picture of a ship—a ship sailing nearly straight towards you. Her prow was gilded

and shaped like the head of a dragon with wide open mouth. She had only one mast and one large, square sail which was a rich purple.  The sides of the ship—what you could see of them where the

gilded wings of the dragon ended—were green.  She had just run up to the top of one glorious blue

wave, and the nearer slope of that wave came down towards you, with streaks and bubbles on it.

She was obviously running fast before a gay wind, listing over a little on her port side. . . All the

sunlight fell on her from that side, and the water on that side was full of greens and purples.  On the

other, it was darker blue from the shadow of the ship.

"The question is," said Edmund, "whether it doesn't make things worse, *looking* at a

Narnian ship when you can't get there."

"Even looking is better than nothing," said Lucy.  "And she is such a very Narnian ship."

The adventure comes to Edmund, Lucy, and their skeptical cousin Eustace Scrubb, when they

realize that the *Dawn Treader* is actually in motion, and the three of them are magically drawn into Narnia

through the picture frame, ending up aboard the ship.  Edmund and Lucy can envision what is about to

happen, but Eustace has no clue—a situation that parallels the experience of many students' entry into

public speaking.  You should be clear about the learning challenges, possibilities, and opportunities

presented by the course.  Your students may be enthusiastic, skeptical, or fearful, but they will all be

uncertain about what lies ahead for them when they walk into your class.


## Teaching Coordinates for the Basic Public Speaking Course

When you enter your classroom, you are more than a mere facilitator—although you will have done

well if you successfully facilitate learning through the entire term.  You are also more than just a

manager—although how you manage the course and the classroom will affect the learning process profoundly.  To teach well, you must be a visionary with a penchant for implementation.  Your students

may harbor some concerns about negotiating the course well.  Therefore, you need both to envision the

course as a whole and to lead students into a concrete, day-by-day learning experience that will seem

adventurous at many points to student and teacher alike.

## Cultivating a Healthy Learning Environment

Think about this question: What do college professors do (or fail to do) that makes a favorable

learning climate impossible or disrupts what would otherwise be a good classroom environment?  Take a

few moments to list specific behaviors that you have seen in college classrooms.  Then consider the

positive side of the same issue: How would you characterize a classroom climate that would best enable

your students to accomplish the objectives you have established for public speaking?  Obviously, the

instructor sets the tone.  The climate should correspond to the content and style in the course.  In particular,

the classroom should promote interaction.  You should make it a safe place—one where people can voice

their opinions in a respectful community, without fear of personal attack (from the instructor or

classmates!).  Students should know that they can make occasional delivery errors without severe

consequences and should leave the course with a better sense of freedom of speech than when the term

began.  At the same time, you want students to recognize the need for them to engage fully in the course

material and class sessions.  They should find a certain intensity and dynamism for learning every time they

come to class.

## *Adapting to Students*

The sheer volume of concepts, theory, and skills deployed in the course are of little consequence to students. Therefore, our chief concern should be what the student needs to know, understand, and do. The means to accomplish this goal resides in connecting with their existing world of experience and knowledge. Forsake visions of pretentious instructors adopting current student attitudes, wardrobe, jargon, etc. Adapting the course material to students can be accomplished in more pedestrian ways, which make the methods more effective.

Here are a few ways to get started adapting the course content to your particular classes. First, students know a great deal about public speaking; they simply lack coordinates and categories to make sense of their knowledge. Start from their context and their terms whenever possible, then move them toward the next order of thinking. Second, tie each class meeting to a project on which they are currently working. Help them to see the conceptual connections to their assignment. *Do not automatically assume that they will see the relationships.* Keep them working on their speech projects and committing, during class time, to choices about how to proceed. Third, work through a sample topic of your own for each speech assignment. By your example and your working with them through the new concepts, they will learn much about your expectations for things like narrowing their topics and adequately supporting their points. Avoid using overly abstract or simplistic topics as hypothetical cases.

## *Modeling Presentation Skills*

Beginning instructors in public speaking tend to feel pressure to perform—literally to practice what they are preaching. We know that students benefit from a good model. However, sticking to a view of students as prospective speakers alone may not be the most helpful approach for teachers.  Instead, think about a different question: What challenges do undergraduates face *as listeners* in a public speaking classroom?

Moving students from a mistake-free performance orientation to one grounded in listener needs should guide your own class presentations.  In other words, should speakers simply try to make an impression, or do they actually have something of substance worth communicating?   If communication is the goal, then you can take initiative in a number of ways that can improve connections between instructors and students.

## Room Arrangement and Proximity

If the room in which you teach has movable seating, consider adjusting the seating arrangement to enhance interaction and keep students in closer proximity to you and one another.  Semi-circular or U-shaped arrangements are particularly effective, even if they need to be two rows deep.  Such arrangements enable you get within one seat of any student, tend to make it easier for students to see visuals and one another, and are conducive to discussion.  Many room arrangements are less than ideal and cannot be easily manipulated.  In less than ideal rooms, work to keep students together in close proximity to you and any visual aids, and maximize your ability to move freely around the room.  By utilizing the classroom space to its fullest, you move the focus of your student listeners and put more people in "front row seats" during the course of the session.  Do not get trapped in the front of the room or in just one spot alone if you can possibly avoid it.

## Agenda

Post a simple agenda for each class session. Students, like any listeners, occasionally fade out and lose focus on the conversation. An agenda will help them stay on track with your remarks and the progress of the session. The agenda can be used strategically to move students along, especially in cases where discussion flourishes, threatening to take over the class session in unproductive ways.

## Eye Contact

Cultivate your ability to maintain direct eye contact with your students throughout each class session. Extemporaneous speaking demands direct eye contact between speakers and listeners—a skill essential to reading and responding to audience feedback during a speech performance. Direct eye contact also contributes to maintaining audience attention, and for instructors it serves as an effective classroom management skill. When students are behaving appropriately, your eye contact communicates your enthusiasm, energy, and personal engagement with students. When students are behaving poorly, a well-placed glare can produce favorable results in a student's ability to listen without disrupting the progress of the session.

## Vocal Variety

Students worry that one characteristic in their voice will produce monotony—speed, pitch, volume, etc. They do not realize that vocal monotony occurs, not because a speaker speaks too quickly, too slowly, too softly, or too loudly, but because one speaks at one pace, one pitch, or one volume. To avoid instructional monotony, avoid long lectures. More important to modeling good presentational practice and classroom effectiveness. plan to use your voice strategically (not melodramatically) to enable students to listen better. Use pauses and welcome silence occasionally.  Remember that *all* variations in speed, pitch, and volume can produce intended emphasis.

## Classroom Audio-Visual Support

Speakers find audio-visual management one of the most important, yet difficult presentation skills to master. Many teachers struggle as well, or seem satisfied with mediocre employment of audio-visual support.  Whether you are using chalk or computer-generated graphics, a cassette player or a sophisticated sound system, you should design, place, and manage your visual aids consistently according to the standards established in your textbook and applied in your evaluation forms for speeches.

## *Incorporating Technology*

As levels of computer literacy and accessibility increase for students, instructors have more options for incorporating technology in the public speaking course. Technological options include presentation software that generates sophisticated visual aids, Internet research capabilities, and speech preparation software.

## Visual Aids

The technological standards for professional presentations have escalated dramatically as laptop computers and LCD projectors have dropped in price. Today, computer-generated images are cutting edge. How and to what degree will you incorporate these technologies into your course? Recognize initially that the application of technology does not immediately make visual aids more effective. The principles for

effective use of visual aids must be in place—the default offerings on some software programs produce

sophisticated color and design options that are substandard for use in performance settings (small type, too

many words per slide, hard-to-read color schemes, excessive detail, etc.). Nevertheless, if accessible to

students, such visual options should be encouraged. The more difficult question has to do with whether or

not you will commit class time to teach a specific software program in the public speaking course. If

institutional resources are not available to students, cost may prohibit many from using high-tech visuals.

Therefore, permitting the use of the most advanced technology is probably good where available.

However, requiring use of computer-generated visuals in public speaking might be unrealistic or unfair.


## Internet Research

The *Allyn & Bacon Quick Guide to the Internet for Speech Communication*, by Terrence A. Doyle,

exemplifies the kind of resources available to help students make the most of the Internet for their public

speaking courses. Myriad web sites expedite the process of finding current information on almost any topic

imaginable.

However, the volume of information does not guarantee the quality. Consider how you can

encourage students to extract sound, reliable, and worthwhile material from the Internet information glut.

Teach them to evaluate Internet sources according to the same sorts of criteria they should be applying to

ordinary sources they might find in the library. What is the reputation of the publisher? Has the material

been subjected to an editorial process? For example, information posted on the Internet about parental

rights by the Associated Press should be taken as more reliable than material on the same topic taken from

Bart Simpson's personal home page. You can lead students into wiser, more efficient use of the Internet in general—not just for your course—by taking some time to outline some basic tenets for web use and holding students accountable to reasonable standards. Also, while Internet research grows in popularity. continue to expect students to utilize the many other good forms of speech research, including interviews. site visits, and traditional library research.

## Lesson Components: Cultivating Interaction With and Between Students

Putting together a good class session combines a number of different factors: knowledge of the topic, good material to make the session meaningful, and the repertoire of instructional skills you possess to develop and execute a learning process that engages your students. If you have been appointed to teach this course, assume that you have access to basic knowledge and good material for the content of the session. Therefore, the remaining aspect of excellent instruction would be how you manage the learning process in the classroom. Effective instructors weave content and process together in ways that appear effortless to students. But the actual weaving is far from effortless. A pivotal presupposition drives our concern with instructional processes: *People learn best when they interact with the material, the instructor, and other learners. Since public speaking, both conceptually and practically, demands consideration and application of human interaction, dynamic classroom interaction should be central to public speaking pedagogy.* Therefore, teaching public speaking well requires adoption of a closely related pedagogical objective: To create a classroom environment in which each student is invited to interact meaningfully with the instructor, classmates, and material.

## *Discussion*

What kinds of things have instructors from your past done that stifled in-class discussion?  A worst-case scenario might be one like the class in which a professor seemed to seek discussion, only to interrupt students in mid-sentence and berate them based on the teacher's inferences (often inaccurate) about what the remainder of the student's response would be.  Straight lecture without opportunity for discussion would probably be better.  But picking on poor practitioners is much simpler than developing good discussion management skills of our own.  To make discussion work better as an instructional tool, use the suggestions that follow.  However, none of the discussion ideas will work effectively until you yourself are convinced that discussion leads to better learning for your students.  If you view discussion primarily as "shared ignorance" or a waste of time, then your discussions will never amount to more than being a charade or filler (and you will probably believe that the bright young minds in your class are dull, thoughtless, and unresponsive).

## Open and Closed Questions

The most important single skill you can learn in discussion management is the difference between an open and a closed question.  Anecdotally, closed questions seem to be the default query for most instructors. Closed questions seek fixed answers, either a yes/no or a single correct answer ("Guess My Answer" questions). The responses are predictable.  And even though the response style does not always accurately represent the turnings of the student mind, the classroom context demands that students obey the conventions in most cases.  For instance, consider the following dialogue as a typical closed-question discussion scenario. The instructor has made some introductory remarks about stage fright and wants to

lead a discussion (statements in parentheses indicate unspoken responses in the minds of the students).

Professor:   Do you fear giving a speech?

Students:   (Yes.)

Professor:   Can anyone tell us about a speaking experience you had and how you dealt with the

nervousness?

Students:   (No.)

Professor:   Well, if you haven't given a speech yourself, are there ways that you have seen other

speakers control their nervousness, or let their nerves take over?

Students:   (Yes.)

Professor:   It seems that you must have mastered the material from the book if you don't want to talk

about it. You're awfully quiet this afternoon. Does anyone have any questions about stage

fright?

Students:   (No.)

Professor:   What does the book say about why stage fright occurs?

Students:   (I think it said something about a natural physiological response to a threatening situation,

but I can't remember exactly—don't want to make a fool of myself today.)

Professor:   OK. Let me list the strategies for managing stage fright on the board.

The professor in this class could go away thinking that the students were disinterested in the class

session, unprepared, or just plain unresponsive. None of these assessments is necessarily accurate. As

students in a classroom context, most people are unwilling to answer fixed alternative questions, even if

they know the answer. This is particularly true of "Guess My Answer" questions, which should be avoided like the plague. In the scenario above, an extrovert might answer each of these questions. but by doing so he or she might well discourage everyone else from participating.

Closed questions are valuable to discussion management. but their primary purpose is to bring discussion to a close or make a transition to another topic. For example, if you want to close a discussion, say, "Does anyone have any other questions or comments?" If a person has an important point to make, he or she will. But in most cases, people will answer "no" in their own minds, say nothing, and allow you to move the session along. Closed questions generally involve "to be" verbs (is, are, was, were, be, being, been), variations on do and can, and any question that presents itself as a "guess my answer" variety.

Open questions invite people into discussion. They allow for many alternative answers. The very way one poses an open question should communicate the expectation for participation. An open question asks for opinions, ideas, examples, or any other sort of response that would enable a number of people to contribute personally. In a classroom setting, open questions should ordinarily be directly on task. For instance, an open question that could lead to significant interaction might go something like this:

Professor:    What kinds of things do people fear might happen when they get up to speak?

Student A:    They might forget what they were going to say.

Student B:    Their voice might crack.

Student C:    They might bore the audience.

Professor:    OK. So we have a variety of reasons why people might fear public speaking. But why would any of these things be a problem in the real world—like in a speech that wasn't being graded?

Student D:    Nobody wants to be embarrassed—there are all those people looking at you!

| | |
|---|---|
| Student A: | Yeah. And if it's a big speech at work, you might lose business or not get a promotion you wanted. |
| Professor: | Any other ideas? |
| Students: | (No.) |
| Professor: | So there are personal and professional consequences we fear if we perform poorly on a speech because of nervousness. Now, let's look at some specific physiological responses associated with the perceived threat of public speaking. (Lecture on physiological aspects of stage fright.) Now that we know that almost everyone experiences stage fright to some degree, that apprehension is tied to our physiological response, what sorts of suggestions have you heard or tried in the past to deal with nervousness in public speaking situations? |

In a process sense, these questions say, "please let us know what you think." The instructor should reinforce that message with tone of voice and other non-verbal indicators as well. By doing so, the students understand that they can think out loud with their classmates about the topic of discussion. They get actively engaged in the learning process without fear of error or reprisal and can make a serious contribution instead. When you are ready to move the discussion along, use a closed question and introduce the next issue.

As you attempt to use open questions to stimulate class discussions, write them out in advance and test them on yourself. Can you come up with multiple good responses? If so, include the questions in your lesson plan. If not, rework them until they meet your test. Initially, always head into the classroom with at least your first few questions prepared. *Then recognize that even well prepared open questions will not prevent extroverts from dominating the discussion unless you employ strategies to include input from the entire class.* The following ideas will enable you to engage the entire class in the thought process and invite a wider variety of students to voice their input as a stimulus to their own learning and the learning of their classmates.

## Writing-Before-Speaking

Picture a class of first graders. Anxious to answer questions in class, many have mastered the technique of raising their hands before the question is even complete, trusting that they will be able to come up with an answer on the spot. Some students never outgrow the practice and will try to answer every question you ask in class. However, many other students can make contributions if you create opportunities for them to gather their thoughts enough to offer a considered response.

Writing-before-speaking is one of the simplest and most effective ways to generate input from a cross-section of students or from each class member. It works on the assumption that almost everyone has something worthwhile to contribute, but that some people need a little more time to consider the issues for discussion—which means that their input is often bypassed. Here is how to use writing-before-speaking. First, let students know that you want them to write, then ask an open question to which you want them to respond. Allow ample time (a minute or so) for them to write a response. Watch until most of the students are done writing. Indicate that you are about to ask for responses. At this point you have a number of good options: (1) ask everyone to give their response (if it is a short answer type of question); (2) select randomly (e.g., everyone born in a certain month); (3) choose a few people who are ordinarily quiet, then open it up for discussion; etc.

By giving students time to write their thoughts, you guarantee that everyone has something to say, so speaking in class becomes less intimidating. It also allows you to include quieter members and to preclude domination of discussion by just a few people. I have also found this to be an excellent method for incorporating a variety of perspectives and maintaining balance in comments from men and women. The writing-before-speaking method need not compel you to hear from everyone on each question, but it does help students to stay engaged mentally and increase their readiness to participate. Once students are engaged in discussion, they also become more responsive and attentive to lecture segments in which the teacher develops ideas and takes students beyond their existing base of knowledge into new material. The principles behind writing-before-speaking allow for variations and use in combination with related methods to stimulate productive classroom discussion.

## Partners and Small Groups

Instead of having students write, you can pose a question and have them discuss it first with a partner. Giving students time to discuss a pertinent question with one another gets each of them engaged, like writing, but also promotes interaction with one another. When you have a pair working together on a question or a problem, you are likely to spawn a number of perspectives and generate a different kind of feedback than when each student writes an individual response. You can poll groups for responses or return to a general discussion.

In some cases, you may decide to begin by asking students to write their own response to your question, but then have them discuss their responses within small groups. This method works particularly well with brainstorming activities—having each individual brainstorm for a minute or two, then create a composite list, and perhaps prioritize the group list before reporting or discussing with the class at large. Sometimes you may choose to limit the discussion primarily to the groups, and then continue with lecture or other activities.

Partner activities and small group discussion provide additional value in the learning process because students interact with the material and one another. Regardless of how many speak in a particular discussion that follows the partner or group activity, their minds are more likely to be stimulated and engaged as learners.

## In-Class Speaking Exercises

Public speaking students need performance training as well as conceptual depth. You can provide some of this training in non-graded experiences. Plan to incorporate some or all of the following sorts of exercises in your course: impromptu speaking, storytelling/example, audience adaptation, citing sources, introductions, and conclusions. In many of these cases, students can practice elements of their speeches that will eventually be performed for a grade. Most students will need to give impromptu speeches in the workplace, and many impromptu skills are transferable to extemporaneous speaking. The rest of the suggestions come directly from concepts and skills students routinely find difficult to execute. By practicing in class, you will help them to perform better and to know what and how to practice more effectively for speeches.

## Group Activities

You will find a wide array of group activities in most public speaking textbooks. Allyn & Bacon includes such ideas in the Instructor's Annotated Editions and teacher's manuals that accompany their student textbooks. You may also find effective activities by talking to other public speaking teachers or you may develop your own activities.  In any case, when you plan to use a group activity in class, make

certain that you:

1.    Define the task clearly for students.

2.    Provide the steps necessary to complete the activity.

3.    Set a time limit.

4.    Establish a reporting mechanism.

Whether you do this on the board, via transparency or computer-generated image, or in a handout,

following these steps will communicate your expectations for the exercise.  Again, when you get students

involved in a good group activity, you get them involved in the learning process and help them to better

engage and process the material.


## *Micro-lectures*

Public speaking class must take students beyond merely awakening and reconfiguring what they

already know.  Therefore, lecturing plays an important role as a component in the classroom learning

process.  The exclusive lecture format has become a stereotype, perhaps because students perceive that such

a format does little to stimulate a love of learning.  But a well-placed and well-performed lecture can

cultivate learning in students in ways that other methods cannot.  Therefore, how instructors incorporate

lecture material into a given class session makes a huge difference.  First, get students engaged in the

session through an introductory question, small group exercise, or other activity.  Second, begin the lecture

with what they already know and proceed into the new ideas or information the lecture is intended to

provide.  Third, limit any single lecture segment to ten minutes or so, after which students should have

opportunity to work with the material in some way.

## *Homework Assignments*

Why include work outside of class as a lesson component?  The quality of learning and participation in class can be greatly enhanced by careful use of assignments outside of class.  For example, do you want your students to be prepared to discuss the reading for the day?  Assign a few discussion questions from the end of the chapter to be collected in class.  *Then use the questions for class discussion!*  Other ideas include:

1.  Ask students to bring in examples for use in class, examples like good and bad evidence, good introductory material, means by which messages can be adapted, good and bad visual aids, examples of appeals to logos, pathos, and ethos.

2.  Incorporate steps of speech design and preparation into outside assignments.  Make it impossible for students to procrastinate on the development of their speeches by requiring them to complete preparation steps as the steps are being taught.  You can configure such assignments in a number of ways, to force students to apply instruction immediately.

3.  Use an outside assignment to debrief their speaking experiences as a lead-in to debriefing a speaking round with the class as a whole.

In all cases, keep your assignments closely tied to the material in the course, binding the conceptual material to the practice and performance aspects of public speaking.

## *Speaking Rounds*

As noted earlier, speaking rounds constitute approximately one half of the class sessions in most courses. Speaking days should be considered instructional days, i.e., lessons. Precious teaching time may be lost if you treat a speaking round as a speech contest, bypassing teaching opportunities in an effort to preserve "fairness" in evaluation. In my experience, grading does not vary in any noticeable way from the beginning to the end of a speaking round, despite in-round instruction. Specifics on speaking rounds will be developed in the next section. For now, keep in mind the value of demonstrating skills, raising questions for the class to consider, and responding to speakers in class with praise, evaluation, and direction. In other words, speaking rounds are prime teaching opportunities. Plan to use them that way.

# Lesson Planning

When you are beginning as a teacher, you need to invest time and energy to move effectively through your first term. A lesson plan can help you to gain certainty about what each class session should accomplish and to gain confidence to implement the plan with skill. Furthermore, committing to a plan puts you in a better position to evaluate what works and what needs to be revised or replaced. Suggestions for how to build a simple, effective lesson plan follow.

## *Residual Message*

What do your students most need to understand by the conclusion of the session? If they could only take one thing from class on that day, what should that one thing be? The one thing you identify is known as a *residual message*. Answer these questions and you will be on the road to a good lesson plan, because teaching public speaking should be more concerned with what students are actually learning than about an instructor somehow covering a certain body of material. At the top of your lesson plan, consider your answers to the questions above and write a complete statement that follows this form: At the end of today's class session, I want each of my students to understand that . . . Here is a sample residual message for a session on introductions, transitions, and conclusions: *At the end of today's class session I want each of my students to understand that introductions, transitions, and conclusions are difficult for speakers to create and to execute well, but they are crucial components to enhance audience attention, understanding, and retention.*

## Specific Objectives

With the overall message in place, turn your attention to the two or three specific instructional goals for the session. For example, teaching a session on introductions, transitions, and conclusions might call for objectives concerning beginning and ending the speech decisively, previewing and reviewing the body of the speech, and helping listeners to make process and content connections between main points. Specific objectives should become your main teaching points, necessary to communicate the residual message of the class session.

## Session Agenda

How will the objectives be addressed in the actual class setting? At this stage you begin to order the concepts and skills you will teach in the session. The session agenda must take into account administrative details and other routine class activities like collecting papers or assigning reading and other outside exercises. Establish a complete agenda for the session and frame it in such a way that you could put the agenda on the board as a guide for students.

## *Working Agenda*

The residual message, objectives, and agenda establish a master plan for the session. Now you need to develop a script or game plan for instruction. With limited time and multiple options to accomplish the day's objectives, you must turn your attention to making decisions about the specific use of lesson components. In other words, you must plan what to do within each agenda item to promote effective learning for students.

## Item

Create a plan for each agenda item. The plan may involve only one activity or a combination of activities. Review the prior segment on lesson components to refresh your memory about a beginning set of options. Write out exactly what you plan to do, including discussion questions, group activities, or lecture notes. If you plan to write something on the board, write down what you want to put on the board and note that you intend to do so.

## Time

Allot class time for each item and write down the allotment on the working agenda. Review the timing for the session as a whole. Allow sufficient time for start-up activity and explanations of assignments, agenda, etc. As you become more accustomed to teaching the course, you will become more accurate in your estimates.  *Remember, speaking exercises, good discussions, and well-designed group exercises take a significant amount of class time.*

## Rationale

Beneath each agenda item, write an instructional rationale for the specific component(s).  Why did you choose to approach the item the way you did?  How do you expect the particular activities in the item to achieve your goals for that agenda item?

## Test for Success

Whenever possible, identify how you can assess the effectiveness of your approach to a particular item after the class is over.  For instance, will you test on this material, will it appear in a speech preparation or evaluation assignment, or in the speech performances themselves?  Not every activity or item will be easy to evaluate and some are impossible, so do not disqualify an instructional activity simply because you cannot figure out a way to evaluate it.  At the same time, recognize that assessment of teaching effectiveness has been gaining importance both for individual instructors and for departments as greater scrutiny is applied to higher education nationwide.

# First Day of Class

Paradoxically, the first day of class for a new instructor is crucial and entirely unimportant.  As a new public speaking instructor, you can be rightfully concerned about how to negotiate the first day of class and start off on the right foot.  On the other hand, no matter what you feel like, the instructional value of the entire term does not depend on how well you handle the first day. After all, many students on your first day roster will not show up for class, and some may well add as late as 10 days into the term. But you will want to get off to a good start, so the following tips are provided to help you approach that first day of class with confidence.

## Making the First Day Count

Plan to use the first class session in its entirety. First impressions are important, and making a good first impression is one of the reasons that new and seasoned instructors may both experience some anticipation on the first day of a new term. The first day provides an opportunity for you to set a positive tone and climate for the course immediately. You will want to build rapport with your students personally, but you should also take advantage of the day to create a favorable learning environment in other ways. Whatever and however you proceed, remember that you can provide instruction and get them involved in learning from the start.

## Ideas and Options

Students should leave the first session with a clear idea of your expectations for their participation and performance in the course. They should also have a sense of the climate you are trying to establish and the basic coordinates they can use to navigate the term successfully. For example, if you want students to interact with you and one another throughout the term, make sure that you include those elements from the start. Are they going to be speaking in this class? If so, get them on their feet, even if only for fifteen seconds each. What do you want them to know about public speaking—both the course and the topic—

before they leave your classroom on day one?  Work it into the lesson plan.  Do you anticipate boring them

to tears each day?  Pass out the syllabus and read it to them aloud in class.

Resist the temptation to have students introduce themselves.  Self-introductions are one of the most

difficult speaking assignments conceivable.  Instead, have students introduce someone in class they have

not met before (they get to know one another immediately), or have them talk about the worst or best

speaker they have seen recently.  Whatever the exercise, make it relevant to public speaking in some clear

way.   Introduce them well to what a class session in the course is like before they ever see a syllabus.  A

conventional way to handle the syllabus is to highlight key issues in it.  Also consider dividing the class up

into groups and assigning each group a page or section of the syllabus, asking them to decide what one

thing is most important for their classmates to know from their assigned segment.  Then open the class for

questions about the syllabus and use the students' points and questions as leads for your comments on

crucial issues in the course.

The first class also provides a natural opportunity for you to introduce your philosophy of teaching

and explain why you are looking forward to the semester.  If you have speaking experience, refer to it in the

first class and remind students that you were not a one-day wonder as a speaker, even if you are quite

polished today.  If you have little public speaking experience yourself, neither apologies nor mentions of

the fact are necessary.  The course was entrusted for you for good reasons.  Proceed on that basis to practice

what you are teaching.


## Planning

Prepare the first session using the same sort of lesson plan discussed previously.  Plan to begin

building the positive learning environment that you envision for the course.  *If you propose to make the class an interactive climate, then get all of the students interacting within the first five minutes!* They will know that you expect them to participate and will be prepared to engage the ideas and skills in the course as long as you continue to lead them through the learning process. (If you start by reading the syllabus, say you want the class to be participatory, and then ask a closed question, at least acknowledge that you are sending mixed messages.)

Allow time on your first day agenda for late arrivals and discussions with students about dropping and adding your course before and after class. Expect that not every student will have a book, even if they all should. Control the room arrangement as well. Orient the seating according to your plan for the term.

Because most public speaking classes are limited in size, you will be in a position to get to know your students by name. Beginning to learn their names on the first day will help you build rapport. Some teachers ask their students to complete index cards with personal information about major, hometown, career goals, and speaking experience. Others greet each student personally, hand out a syllabus, and write down the students' name as a means of taking roll on the first day. Whatever your strategy, establish a plan to start learning names and dealing with your students on a personal level.

## *Performing*

Teaching is a performance. Instructors are not entertainers, but sound instruction includes elements of performance which contribute to the sense of anticipation you will feel as the first day of class approaches. Enjoy the performance. Recognize that you are participating in an ancient educational ritual, teaching a course in which you can help your students gain a competency that will stay with them throughout their lives. Public speaking *is* critical to maintaining the democratic freedoms cherished by Americans. The first day of class provides you with an opportunity to invite students into a new, sometimes fearful, but rewarding venture. Your performance will set the pace for them, and in the first performance you begin to enact for them what you have planned for the course to become for them as individuals and as a class.

# Speaking Rounds

The instructional value of a speaking round has been mentioned, but not developed. As we mentioned early in the book, public speaking is a performance course. Therefore, we need to consider the aspects of pedagogy related to performance, namely, the speaking rounds. Do not confuse teaching about how to design a speech with performance instruction. If you choose to remove your teacher's hat during speaking rounds and don only a judge's cap, you will have abdicated many wonderful instructional opportunities. Of course, by using both caps in a speaking round you accept some tricky dynamics. But if we profess to be more concerned with learning than with grading, we must accept this set of difficulties.

## *Speech Days as Teaching Opportunities*

The teaching opportunities come when students are thinking about the most important parts of public speaking while they listen to their classmates and perform their own speeches. Part of your job is to keep them involved in the process each day of the speaking round. Be prepared to raise germane questions and to entertain the questions of your students. The inquiry may occur in the open classroom, through your evaluations or peer evaluations, or come from student reviews of their own performances (using videotape). However, students are not likely to view speaking rounds as learning opportunities unless you prompt them to do so by your words and actions.  Build up speaking days as the highlight of the course and push

your students to stay engaged in the process throughout, especially when they are not assigned to speak.

## *Variations on Speaking Round Formats*

Choose speaking round formats that fit best with your instructional objectives.  People structure

speaking rounds in widely divergent ways depending on what they are trying to accomplish.  For example,

some teachers provide all the instruction necessary to complete a series of four speeches, finishing all

reading, non-speaking round class sessions, and testing in the first half of the term.  Students present their

speeches for remainder of the term.  Another, more common approach, brings students together in a large

lecture format for instruction on the conceptual basis of public speaking and speech design.  Students are

divided into lab sections in which to present their speeches.  Most people who are assigned a section of

public speaking, whether as a professor, lecturer, instructor, or graduate instructor, work with speaking

rounds interspersed between conventional instructional sessions throughout the term.  This would mean, for

example, a model in which instruction on informative speaking is followed by an informative speech, then

instruction on persuasive speaking is followed by a persuasive speech, and so on.

Assuming a model like the one noted above, with a discrete speaking round for a particular kind of

speech, instructors have a number of options for structuring a round.  The first choice to make is how to

handle the sequence of speeches.  Some teachers allow students assigned to a given day to speak

consecutively, and then provide commentary for all at the end of class.  This method assures that time will

permit all speakers to complete their speeches with plenty of time remaining in the class session.  The

instructor can be selective about comments and can address certain global issues evident in more than one

of the speeches.  Student comments, if included in the process, can be somewhat depersonalized.

A second, recommended, approach sets aside a certain amount of time for each speaker, including the performance and feedback time. For example, a five-minute speech would take about ten minutes of class time with commentary. Therefore, a class of 24 students would require six speaking days. Using this approach, speakers present their speeches and receive immediate feedback before the next student proceeds. Each student receives individual attention from teacher and classmates, and the performance can be used as an instructional tool for the entire group, keeping a focus on the issues at hand concerning public speaking. When something particularly good happens, the instructor can commend it. When a common difficulty emerges in a performance—especially one that all need to work at or understand better—the teacher can consider it with the class constructively.

Taking speeches one at a time with commentary allows for a number of options during the comment period. In every case, assume that the instructor will take the lead on oral feedback. The options include:

1. Will students complete written evaluations? (All students or a selected group may write peer evaluations.)

2. Will students provide oral feedback? Will student feedback include constructive criticism or be limited to positive elements of the presentation?

3. Will speakers respond to Q& A? (A good idea in at least some rounds, since Q & A sessions are the rule in most public presentations and because human discourse expects a response.)

Each speaking round may be different, and probably should be, since the instructional objectives for each speaking round should be different. The time constraints must be carefully observed to make sure that all the speeches planned for the day can be presented. Choose some means of keeping students who are not speaking involved, whether writing comments, providing oral feedback, or raising questions.

## *Preparing Teacher and Students*

Students should never be surprised by what transpires in the speaking round process.  Establish a routine and explain it clearly to students, including what you expect from students who are not speaking on a given class day.

## *Speech Evaluations*

Public speaking instructors must develop a unique pedagogical skill: grading speeches.  Speech evaluations require more than assigning a grade.   But learning how to assess a speech, assign a grade, and *justify the grade* to yourself and your students constitutes one of the greatest challenges for new instructors. This segment breaks down the process of evaluation into more manageable parts.

### Summative and Formative Evaluation

First, understand that a good speech evaluation includes both a summative evaluation , a grade, and formative evaluation—comments to help the student improve their next performance.  The summative evaluation is your judgment.  You coach through formative evaluation.  Most of the concerns speech instructors harbor regarding evaluation evaporate when both types of evaluation are practiced with care.

### How to Assign a Grade

Justifying speech grades seems particularly difficult because "subjectivity" seems such an easy charge to make.  Students should be gently reminded that the course mimics life outside of the classroom.

in which audiences all respond to speeches subjectively, but still make evaluations that routinely change the course of personal lives and occasionally change the course of history.

Clarify your standards; teach students how to meet your standards, and grade according to criteria that match your standards. The most effective way to ease student concerns about the speech grading process is to evaluate students according to criteria for generally discernable elements of the speech process *that you teach them to perform in preparation for the speech.* For example, if you expect them to include a preview of their main points in the introduction to their speech, teach them what a preview is and explain the range of acceptable performance behaviors. ("You don't need to say, *my first main point is... my second main point is... my third main point is....* But you must somehow make your main points clear enough that a careful listener could write them down.") Then include the presence and quality of a preview in the evaluation criteria. The same goes for visual aids, supporting material, audience adaptation, structure, reasoning, etc.

Students worry most about delivery. They worry that teachers will downgrade them heavily because they cannot win the class fashion contest, or have a squirrelly voice, or have trouble making eye contact. Like everything else, delivery should be included in the criteria, but once students realize that you can tell whether they organized their speeches well and use good sources—even if their knees are knocking the whole time—most will relax about grading. In reality, most of the things we want them to do can be done well, even with some delivery snafus. Eventually, they will understand that the smooth talker with poor organization and little substance could get a *D*, while someone who prepared and presented an outstanding message but lacked gestures and was still working against vocal monotony could get into the *A* range.

In addition to formulating specific criteria, provide a global sense of what students need to do to achieve a certain grade.  For example, if a student includes every required element, but without any distinction or creativity, that should place him or her in the *C* range.  A speech oozing with creativity and energy, but lacking in a few areas, might be a *B*, and so on.  Whatever sort of evaluation form you use, document what did and did not happen in the speech according to your criteria.  Then aim for strict consistency in how you apply the standards.  Soon, you will develop a feel for the grade range in which a speech belongs and have full confidence in explaining both how the student earned the grade *and how she or he might improve the next performance to get to a higher level.*

## Writing Comments

The quality and tone of your written comments concerning the speech probably play a role as important in student perceptions of grading fairness as defining and documenting evaluation standards.  Make sure to include space on your evaluation form for *formative* comments.  In fact, all your written comments other than your notes taken during the speech should be coaching comments, things that worked well in the performance and suggestions for improvement on the next one.

Note as many areas of success and identifiable potential as you can.  Each can be mentioned briefly.  But feel no compulsion to mention every problem you observe.  You neither have time, nor can you stimulate much positive progress by doing so.  When addressing problems, stick to two or three issues.  As in many skill-training situations, correcting one major problem may solve many others.  For instance, poorly managed note cards often cause poor eye contact, reduce the speaker's animation of expression and gesture, and result in vocal monotony.  Dealing with the note management problem may strengthen the performance in a number of ways.  Time management problems point to underdeveloped research, poor structure, lack of focus and discrimination in message development, or poor practice habits. Think about the root cause, limit your comments to that problem, and minimize or omit commentary on the time issue (even though the student may have lost points to speaking to briefly or too long).

Regardless of the grade, you should make suggestions that demonstrate genuine concern for helping the student to improve as a speaker. Even *A* speeches allow you to take students to new levels of performance, urging them to explore new territory in delivery or to attempt different speech structures or strategies. In this way, your students will come to appreciate your knowledge of public speaking and personal attention. Therefore, you may well soften the reality of a low grade by providing multiple insights that prove you do not cast them in one grade range without any hope for a higher grade.

## Responding as a Listener

In addition to evaluative comments, include a personal response to the message in every written evaluation. Demonstrate that you were being attentive to more than the criteria, and respect the student as a speaker in his or her own right. A speech may spark a memory, a thought, or a question. You may share an experience about yourself that the student could not have known. In persuasive speeches, you may agree, disagree, raise related issues for you, etc. This is also the place where you can register your listening enjoyment and appreciation. You elevate the significance of the speaking event and humanize your classroom by doing so.

## Grading and Videotape

Nothing builds credibility for your speech evaluation skill like videotaping student speeches. If possible, videotape every speech. Have students supply their own tapes and do not review the tape yourself. Record the speeches for students' benefit. Videotaping provides a wonderful opportunity for students to grow through self-evaluation. In my experience, videotape also radically alters student perceptions of the quality of speech evaluations from their teachers. The predominant comment instructors get from students goes something like this, "When I saw your evaluation of me, I didn't think that I had done the things you said; then I watched it and I couldn't believe it. Everything you wrote was true and I thought you were actually too easy on me." Although this rarely happens, if a student ever claimed that a teacher had missed an element in a speech, they could review the tape together and clarify the situation.

# Testing

Will you include tests in your course? If so, why and how? Most public speaking textbook instructor's manuals provide test questions. Some provide test bank software. The question of how to incorporate testing into your course cannot be solved by these resources. The reasons why you test will help you determine the type, frequency, and development of your quizzes, tests, or exams.

## *Objectives*

Tests can play a number of different instructional roles. We most commonly think of tests as a means of assessing conceptual understanding in students. But tests can also be used as a learning tool and as a simple means to prompt students to keep up with their reading. You may use exams for any or all of these purposes in public speaking. However you incorporate testing into your course, identify your objective and keep it in mind during test design.

# Types

Multiple choice, true-false, short-answer, and essay questions are conventional and serviceable kinds of items for traditional in-class examinations to assess conceptual understanding. Obviously, a test can be constructed of all one sort of test item or of some combination. Your choices will affect the length of time students need to complete the test and the kinds of assessment the test will provide.

Because of limited class time and the nature of the material, take-home exams are well suited to the public speaking course. For instance, exams in which students are asked to make choices that help them understand speech design process or how to build a good argument can be done at home, open-book, and advance the learning process beyond what the constraints of class time allow.

Testing for reading comprehension also places a premium on learning outside of class. Students habitually neglect textbook reading. Tests to push them into the text motivate them to explore the benefits offered in texts—like the many examples, applications, and fine points on public speaking—that cannot and should not be covered during class time. *Once students discover that they will be accountable for the reading assignments, they read, and do so much more carefully.*

# Frequency

If you are testing for conceptual understanding, test at natural unit breaks during the term. From this standpoint, a mid-term and a final would be sufficient, although you may choose to give an additional exam or two. If you are using a take-home test as a learning tool, it should correspond with the specific topic or process you want students to learn. Take-home tests require more grading time, so use them sparingly unless you have time to burn. Reading comprehension tests or quizzes should be simple to give, take, and grade. They should be more frequent, because students should be urged to keep up with the reading. Allowing too much time between such tests tempts students to fall behind on their reading.

## *Development*

With your objective in mind, construct your exam to accomplish your purposes. Remember these basic tenets:

1.  *Value the test and the items within the test equitably.* Consider using five point values whenever possible. Five or more points per item will result in clearer distinctions between scores when you grade the test and will prevent many complaints over "just one point."

2.  *Remember the time constraints within which your students must complete the test.* Whether you test in class or give a take-home test, avoid frustrating students by giving them too much test for the time allotted.

3.  *Assume that if you give them a test that is an easy mark, students will be tempted to cheat.* Create two versions of the test with identical questions, but put the questions on different pages. Such adjustments are simple in the age of word processing.

4.  *Whatever you construct must be graded.* Especially be careful to assign only the essay questions to which you are willing to devote much time. Also, to ease and speed the grading process, ask short-answer questions with definitive answer components.

# Chapter Four:
# Dealing with Challenges

How do you expect your public speaking teaching to affect your attitudes and performance in other responsibilities?  Where do you expect to find healthy integration?  Where do you expect to experience tension?  In this chapter, we will consider how best to navigate the course as one responsibility among many in the instructor's life.  For example, some new instructors focus narrowly on the content of the course and the teaching performance within each class meeting, neglecting other pedagogical matters which are just as important as in-class instruction.  Such everyday teaching challenges frequently arise for new instructors.  Some are unavoidable, while other problems teachers invite upon themselves.  By preventing or anticipating their emergence, you can negotiate these challenges and turn many into opportunities.

## Teaching With Limited Speaking Experience

If you have been appointed to teach public speaking, a lack of personal experience in public speaking would naturally make your entry into the classroom more challenging.  If you find yourself in this situation, remember that you are teaching the course because the department believes you are qualified.  Your best qualification may be your ability to learn the material quickly and completely enough to stay two steps ahead of the class.  In your first few terms, you can teach students how to learn by learning with them.  Still, you are probably more concerned about performance than conceptual material.  First, your classroom itself serves as a routine opportunity for you to develop speaking experience.  Include a well-prepared lecture as part of each class session and treat it as a formal presentation from your perspective.  The students need not have any indication of what you are doing, but you can build confidence quickly, both as a speaker and an instructor by practicing *as* you preach. Second, look for opportunities to speak outside of the classroom context. Whether you join a toastmasters club or seek out and accept speaking engagements, try to get more "real world" experience giving speeches.

## Integrating Teaching and Coursework

If you are a graduate student with a teaching appointment, tension between your roles and responsibilities as teacher and student are inevitable. Both roles require good performance to maintain your status. You must find ways to *teach your strengths*. By doing so, you will prepare your lessons with greater efficiency and pleasure. While you should not alter the syllabus radically, teach the material from perspectives most familiar to you. For example, if you are studying organizational communication, bring that emphasis to the public speaking context. If you are studying political communication, by all means introduce speeches and other kinds of political presentations as examples. If you study small group communication, incorporate a group project and presentation. If you study argumentation, pay particular attention to teaching strong argument skills through the course. Obviously, the syllabus must still include the basics of public speaking, but bring the best of your knowledge into the classroom where it fits, and see if you can do so without getting caught! If on any given day you see your teaching responsibilities as a necessary evil, take a mental health day and relax a bit. If you develop a persistent attitude toward teaching as merely a vehicle to keep you in school, or as a take-it-or-leave-it enterprise, do yourself and your students a favor and get out of the field entirely.

# Time Management

Teaching has long been considered a profession. As a professional, you are accountable for your own time, which brings a wealth of potential for freedom, flexibility, and frustration. Looking at how you manage your time can often tell you how well you are managing your teaching, especially in reference to your other responsibilities. If you are an adjunct, your duties may already be well defined and your time available for the public speaking course may be set. However, many new instructors must balance a full load of graduate courses and teach two sections of public speaking. The following time management suggestions apply to both adjuncts and graduate students, but are particularly important for teachers with more discretion in their schedules:

1. **Always return speech evaluations at the next scheduled class session.** To lose credibility and destroy rapport, be chronically late in returning speech evaluations. To maintain the respect of your students and your own sanity, commit yourself to grading speeches from each session before the next session. For the same reasons, *commit to a return date for other graded assignments* (not necessarily the next class session).

2. **Allow 15 minutes per speech on written evaluations.** Work to get under 10 minutes per speech. Students need you to identify their problem areas and point them toward how to improve. They need a brief response to the content of their speeches. What you can write in the first ten minutes is probably what will help them to improve most.

3. **Block out a routine time in your schedule for lesson planning and grading.** Make the block large enough for heavy days. Better to have time left over than to neglect either instructional duties or other responsibilities.

4.  **Use office hours for public speaking administrative work.** Update your grade book, review simple assignments, make arrangements for audio/visual equipment, set up a speaking order; whatever administration the course requires, plan to use office hours to accomplish the mindless tasks. Some days a number of students will visit, but other days you will have the whole time to yourself. Do course-related work that permits interruption.

5.  **Never procrastinate on non-public speaking duties by spending unplanned time on the course.** People who enjoy teaching and struggle with coursework or research can be prone to devote themselves more fully to pedagogical concerns than they should, using course preparation as a rationalization for neglecting other responsibilities. Not surprisingly, teaching provides immediate gratification when students are responsive and growing through the term. Coursework and research tend to require greater perseverance, and produce fruit at a slower pace. Therefore, people who know better may still spend too much time on teaching, to their own detriment. Keep your public speaking time in perspective.

## Student Problems

During the upcoming term:

♦ one student will profess intense fear of public speaking;

♦ another student will become clinically depressed;

♦ many will experience the death of grandparents;

♦ a number will claim that they will lose a scholarship if a grade is not elevated;

♦ some will miss weeks of class with mononucleosis; and

♦  a few will become course design critics.

Ordinarily, no section of the public speaking course will have more than two or three of such cases, but it is hard to predict which ones will surface. Here are a few tips on how to deal with each of these commonplace student problems:

1.  **Apprehension:** When students fear that they will not be able to perform at all because of speaking apprehension, take them seriously. If the following conditions are true in your course (and they should be) reinforce them with an apprehensive student:  a) everyone experiences some apprehension as they learn to speak in public; b) most people fear delivery aspects of the course; c) delivery is not nearly the most important criteria for grading, especially in the early speeches; d) the type of public speaking they will be learning (extemporaneous) will help them not to have to worry about forgetting their main ideas or losing their place in the speech;  e) you can help them as they work through the speech design process and practice their speeches before presenting them in class.

Occasionally, students experience such severe apprehension that they may need to be assigned to a special section of the course, if available at your institution. However, with encouragement and help, most students can succeed in the course, especially if you demonstrate creativity and flexibility in dealing with such cases.

2.  **Mental Health Issues:** Because public speaking classes tend to be smaller than many, especially at large universities, students may come to you with personal difficulties. You must discern whether these are relatively routine matters or larger issues. For instance, romance problems are one thing, but if a student begins to talk about involvement in an abusive relationship, help is needed beyond what most instructors are trained to provide. Know the numbers for the counseling professionals at

your institution and do not hesitate to refer students. In fact, be prepared to be a resource to provide the link students may need to get help.

3.  **Personal/Family Matters:** If a student claims that a grandparent has died, believe it. Never ask for an obituary. Traditional college students are at a stage of life in which grandparents die and other family issues routinely emerge. In one semester, I had three freshmen students, the youngest in their families, each of whom had parents divorce the month after college started. Instructors are better off allowing themselves to be conned in such situations than to challenge wrongly a single grieving student. Offer help to such students by urging them to report their situation to academic advisors or whoever notifies teachers officially concerning excused absences for such reasons, and extend as much flexibility as possible to help these students to complete their coursework.

4.  **Grades:** Certain students need to maintain a set grade point average (GPA) to meet a variety of goals. You should proceed with your grading oblivious to these individual matters. At the end of the semester, a student or two may arrive in your office saying, "If I don't get a ___ in this class, I will not be . . ." They may ask for special opportunities for extra credit to raise the grade. Students may question an earlier grade (and if you have instituted a sensible grade complaint policy, you will have an easy answer and rationale). A few brazen souls may request special consideration and make a case for raising the grade simply because of their situation. Remember that the grade in public speaking is rarely, if ever, the only grade in question. Unless you make a calculation error in the course grade, the responsibility for the mark lies squarely with the student. Do not fall for the pathetic appeal.

5.  **Illness:** Again, traditional students operate in patterns and living situations that seem to make them more susceptible to illness. Instructors should attempt genuine flexibility and generosity in such

cases, but primarily with students who deal responsibly with participation and attendance by promptly informing you when they must be absent and by working hard to make up missed work. You can appropriately ask for some sort of documentation from people who give evidence of abusing the excuse. Producing a note from a doctor or a health center is not nearly so traumatic as being asked to produce an obituary to prove a loved one's death.

6.  **Course Complaints:** Every so often a student may come to your office and explain to you how the course should be taught. These students may actually believe they are the last hope for saving you from yourself. They may have a problem with your classroom manner, the textbook, the number of speeches, other assignments, or any number of other aspects of the course. Check your impulse to correct such students quickly. Listen carefully. You may gain unexpected insights into how students experience the course. In most cases, a student's distress is real and the course is a part of the stress. That does not mean that you should necessarily adopt any of the suggestions. But by listening first and refusing to take offense at the many offensive things such students are capable of interjecting, you may gain insight into yourself as an instructor and the course. Plus, you may help the student to perform better and learn more, even if conditions do not change dramatically.

# Instructor Pitfalls

What difficulties can you avoid? The potential pitfalls are many, and few are exclusive to inexperienced instructors. But the routine pitfalls surround student rapport, classroom management, and teaching tangents.

## Student Rapport

Most people want to be liked. As new instructors, many of us are tempted to make a priority of being liked by our students. We want our students to trust us and enjoy our class, a pretty natural response when trying on a new role for size. Instructors without much distance from their own undergraduate days feel the tension between acceptance and authority most keenly. Of course, students should not despise their instructor—that is not the point. But work to win student approval *as their instructor*. Follow this rule: If all of your students like you all of the time, you are probably not challenging them enough.

You can select from a variety of strategies to focus your relationship with students on your student-teacher interaction. Consider symbolic issues like your wardrobe, how students can contact you, how you prefer to be addressed, and your language. You may feel uncomfortable initially having students call you *Ms.* or *Mr.* On the other hand, you may feel less comfortable at the end of the term when a student comes in and challenges a grade on a first name basis. But whatever you decide about these issues, do not make the error of socializing with your students during the semester in other than official contexts. Develop your social relationships with graduate students if you are a graduate student and with other faculty members if you are an adjunct professor. Also develop social relationships with people off campus.

## Getting Behind on Speech Grading

**Commit yourself to return speech grades at the class meeting following a student's speech.** Students invest much emotional energy when they prepare a speech. Typically, they pay close attention to the time it takes for you to return their speech evaluations. They deserve a predictable turnaround time on their performance evaluations. Fair or not, in my experience students employ prompt return of their speech evaluations as a litmus test concerning the competence of their instructor. In particular, instructors who lack diligence in this one area of grading seem to experience the swiftest, most serious loss of respect from students.

## Student Misdemeanors

When students behave inappropriately in class, how will you handle it? Avoid embarrassing students, even if they may have earned the embarrassment. Instead, use the return of a written assignment to send a message concerning minor problems. A brief, direct e-mail message may also have a favorable effect. During class, move to a quick group activity and divide problem pairs or sets of students by placing them in different work groups. If student conflict flares up (i.e., verbal conflict) avoid taking sides and emphasize process control and rules for civil dialogue. In other words, avoid direct personal confrontation as much as possible. If necessary, arrange a meeting after class.

## Course Process Comments

Avoid making process comments about your own attitude toward the course, especially if you are operating within a structured syllabus designed by the course director. You need not like the design. But voice your personal concerns about the course structure or policies to the director or department chair. You in no way benefit your students by voicing your concerns to them.

## *Using Public Speaking as a Front*

Occasionally, instructors who would prefer to be teaching another communication course—perhaps a theory course, criticism course, or some other area of specialty. Whether you work from a departmental syllabus or develop your own, teach public speaking. You may gain greater satisfaction by teaching your favorite material, but your students will not be well served. Yes, teach your strengths, but teaching your strengths does not equal using the public speaking course as a front for the course you most aspire to teach.

## *Ideological Pulpiteering*

Will you seek to help your students to find their public voices, or do you expect them to parrot *your* public voice? A recent conference panel I attended in a closely-related field featured a series of speakers who advocated the use of a similar introductory course to proselytize students to a particular ideological position. The panel suggested that readings, assignments, and class discussions be used as a means for "consciousness raising" among impressionable students. Own your perspectives. Do not allow yourself to be constrained by the status quo. Challenge your students with new perspectives that might provoke new ideas and cultivate critical thinking. But resist the temptation to use the course for your personal political purposes.

# Free Speech Issues

How do you deal with a student who wants to advocate a position that you find problematic for one reason or another? First, you are responsible for the classroom, and the classroom should both stimulate learning and approximate real-world circumstances.  Respect the mission of the institution in which you teach, regarding your classroom, policies on speech topics.  Second, you may rightly insist that your students not promote violation of the law in your classroom and prescribe other constraints on props and visual aids (for instance, no firearms or facsimiles thereof).

Religious speeches may pose one of the most vexing problems for public speaking instructors. Regardless of your personal religious convictions (or lack thereof), religious speeches need not raise such concerns, and the freedom of speech for a student committed to a religious topic need not be violated. Simply structure your assignments to make a simplistic religious speech that would seek to proselytize a captive audience a poor selection.  Then welcome a religious topic that satisfies the assignment.  Most religious students will accurately read a prohibition against all religious speech as a violation of the First Amendment.  But if you guide a student from a weak approach to the assignment to a stronger way to address the assignment with a religious topic of their choosing, they may well respond with a presentation satisfactory to both student and instructor.

# Chapter Five:
# Resource Matrix

As a public speaking instructor, one of the most practical issues you face is planning engaging

lessons for your students.  Each of the four Allyn & Bacon public speaking textbooks are available in

instructor's annotated editions (IAEs) and are accompanied by instructor's manuals, both of which supply

ideas for exercises, activities, and test items.

Earlier in this manual, I noted the importance of teaching your strengths and, as a new instructor in

the public speaking course, you may benefit greatly by looking at how other A&B textbooks, training

manuals, and support materials present the same topics covered in your primary textbook.  Additionally,

A&B has produced a full range of resources designed to enhance the outside-of-class learning experience

for your students.  Below is a comprehensive list of A&B resources and supplemental materials available

for you and your students, followed by a matrix showing the correlation between chapters in A&B texts and

instructors manuals plus the supporting materials.

## Allyn & Bacon Public Speaking Texts

### Public Speaking: An Audience-Centered Approach, Third Edition

Steven A. Beebe, Southwest Texas State University

Susan J. Beebe, Southwest Texas State University

This text's distinctive audience-centered approach is the major theme that guides the speaker

through the speechmaking process by emphasizing the importance of analyzing and considering the

audience at every point along the way. Numerous examples, excerpts, and sample speeches support the instruction. Featured narratives by professionals, "Speakers at Work," exemplify ways to adapt and succeed in challenging scenarios.  Information on adapting to diverse audiences, a chapter on ethics, and technology for research and visual aid preparation equip students to manage public speaking throughout their professional lives.

## *Public Speaking in the Age of Diversity, Second Edition*

Teri Kwal Gamble, College of New Rochelle

Michael W. Gamble, New York institute of Technology

In their age-of-diversity treatment of public speaking, the authors' reflect their view that public speaking is a bridge to change in attitudes, beliefs, values, and behavior.  This text addresses these issues by providing a complete teaching-learning package that promotes active student participation in the learning process.  Theme features include "Considering Diversity" and "Speaking of Critical Thinking." "Speaking of Skill Building" and the "Speaker's Stand," are hands-on exercises and activities designed to help students focus their attention and practice public speaking skills.

## *Mastering Public Speaking, Third Edition*

George L. Grice, Radford University

John F. Skinner, San Antonio College

This text uses a casual and engaging style to guide students through  the speechmaking process. The authors emphasize critiquing speech through the observation and analysis of public speaking examples, excerpts, and sample speeches. The "Speaker's Journal," consisting of a series of interviews with a student speaker at various points in the speechmaking process, examines his self-critiquing process. Another theme, the ethical contract between speaker and audience, is provided through a separate chapter on ethics and Ethical Decisions" boxes, aimed at stimulating thoughtful classroom debates on the difficult choices facing public speakers and listeners.

### *Public Speaking: Strategies for Success, Second Edition*

David Zarefsky, Northwestern University

Zarefsky encourages students to think through and about their strategies in the public speaking process. Students are urged to consider the diversity of audiences, occasions, and speakers, and to choose a specific purpose, a relevant topic, and the appropriate material to make their speeches successful. "Applying Strategies" boxes illustrate how students can apply the strategies approach to speaking. "Choose a Strategy" boxes build upon concepts and skills introduced by asking students to apply a strategy to various speaking situations.

## Allyn & Bacon Supplemental Materials

### *Speech Preparation Workbook*

Jennifer Dreyer and Gregory H. Patton, San Diego State University

This helpful workbook takes your students through the various stages of speech creation-from audience analysis to writing the speech-and provides guidelines, tips, and easy-to-fill-in pages.

## *Public Speaking in the Multicultural Environment, Second Edition*

Devorah A. Lieberman

This essay is an effort to help students think about the effects the diverse backgrounds of the members can have. not just on how speeches are prepared and delivered. but also on how those speeches are perceived.  It will help them learn to analyze the cultural diversities within their audience(s) and provide them with specific tools to adapt their presentations.

## *Preparing Visual Aids for Presentations*

Dan Cavanaugh

This booklet is designed to introduce students to the art of using a computer to prepare effective graphics for their speeches.  It includes strategies for using visuals in conjunction with a presentation, general guidelines for effective designs, and an introduction to the use of PowerPointTM.

| Topic | Beebe & Beebe | Gamble & Gamble | Grice & Skinner | Zarefsky | PowerPoint™ Transparency | Allyn & Bacon Supplements |
|---|---|---|---|---|---|---|
| Introduction to Public Speaking | 1 Appendix A | 1 | 1 | 1 | T1, T4-7 | |
| Ethics and Public Speaking | 3 | 3 | 2 | | | |
| Diversity and Public Speaking | 1 | Integrated Throughout | | | | *Public Speaking in the Multicultural Environment* |
| Speech Design Process | 2 | 2 | 3 | 4 | T11-12, T19-20 | |
| Speaking Apprehension | 2 | 2 | 3 | 1 | T2-3 | |
| Listening | 4 | 4 | 4 | 2 | T8-10 | |
| Audience Analysis | 5 | 5 | 5 | 3 | T13-18 | Speech Preparation Workbook, pp. 1-13 |
| Topic Selection | 6 Appendix B | 6 | 6 | 4 | T21-25 | Speech Preparation Workbook, pp. 14-21 |
| Researching the Topic | 7 | 7 | 7 | 5 | T26-27 | Speech Preparation Workbook, pp. 22-31 |
| Using the Internet | 7 | 7 | 7 | Integrated Throughout | | *Quick Guide to the Internet for Speech Communication* |
| Supporting the Message | 8 | 8 | 8 | 6 | T28-31 | Speech Preparation Workbook, pp. 32-39 |
| Organizing the Body of the Speech | 9 | 9 | 9 | 7 | T32-33 | Speech Preparation Workbook, pp. 40-48 |
| Introductions, Conclusions, and Transitions | 10 | 10 | 10 | 8 | T37-43 | Speech Preparation Workbook, pp. 58-68 |
| Outlining | 11 | 11 | 11 | 9 | T34-36 | Speech Preparation Workbook, pp. 49-57 |
| Language | 12 | 12 | 12 | 10 | T54-57 | |
| Delivery | 13 | 13 | 13 | 11 | T44-53 | Speech Preparation Workbook, pp. 82 |
| Visual Aids | 14 | 14 | 14 | 12 | T80-100 | *Preparing Visual Aids for Presentations* |
| Using PowerPoint9 | Appendix C | | | | | |
| Informative Speaking | 15 | 15 | 15 | 13 | T58-59 | Speech Preparation Workbook, pp. 70-71 |
| Persuasive Speaking | 16 | 16 | 16 | 14 | T60-67 | Speech Preparation Workbook, pp. 72-76 |
| Reasoning | 17 | 8,16 | 17 | 6 | T68-74 | COMPREHENSIVE SUPPLEMENTS: |
| Ceremonies and Special Occasions | 18 | 17 | 18 | 15 Appendix A | T75-76 | A &B Public Speaking Website |
| Small Group Speeches | 19 | 18 | 19 | 15 | T77-79 | SoundGuide for Public Speaking Interactive Speechwriter Software, v. 1.1 |
| Speech Criticism and Analysis | 3 | 4 | 4 | 2 | | |
| Sample Speech Texts | Appendix D | | Appendix | Appendix B | | Allyn & Bacon Student Speeches Video Library |

NOTES

NOTES

NOTES

NOTES

NOTES

NOTES

NOTES

# NOTES

NOTES